Christian Morality

FRAMEWORKS
Interdisciplinary Studies for Faith and Learning

Previously published
volumes in the series:

What's So Liberal about the Liberal Arts?
Integrated Approaches to Christian Formation

Paul W. Lewis and
Martin William Mittelstadt, editors

Christian Morality

An Interdisciplinary Framework for Thinking about Contemporary Moral Issues

EDITED BY
Geoffrey W. Sutton
and
Brandon Schmidly

PICKWICK Publications • Eugene, Oregon

CHRISTIAN MORALITY
An Interdisciplinary Framework for Thinking about Contemporary Moral Issues

Frameworks: Interdisciplinary Studies for Faith and Learning

Copyright © 2016 Wipf and Stock Publishers. All rights reserved. Except for brief quotations in critical publications or reviews, no part of this book may be reproduced in any manner without prior written permission from the publisher. Write: Permissions, Wipf and Stock Publishers, 199 W. 8th Ave., Suite 3, Eugene, OR 97401.

Pickwick Publications
An Imprint of Wipf and Stock Publishers
199 W. 8th Ave., Suite 3
Eugene, OR 97401

www.wipfandstock.com

PAPERBACK ISBN: 978-1-4982-0476-7
HARDCOVER ISBN: 978-1-4982-0478-1
EBOOK ISBN: 978-1-4982-0477-4

Cataloguing-in-Publication data:

Names: Sutton, Geoffrey W., editor. | Schmidly, Brandon, editor.

Title: Christian morality : an interdisciplinary framework for thinking about contemporary moral issues / edited by Geoffrey W. Sutton and Brandon Schmidly.

Description: Eugene, OR : Pickwick Publications, 2016 | Series: Frameworks: Interdisciplinary Studies for Faith and Learning | Includes bibliographical references.

Identifiers: ISBN 978-1-4982-0476-7 (paperback) | ISBN 978-1-4982-0478-1 (hardcover) | ISBN 978-1-4982-0477-4 (ebook)

Subjects: LSCH: Christian ethics.

Classification: BJ1249 .C43 2016 (paperback) | BJ1249 .C43 (ebook)

Manufactured in the U.S.A.   07/29/16

Unless otherwise indicated, all Scripture quotations are from the New Revised Standard Version Bible. New Revised Standard Version Bible, copyright © 1989 the Division of Christian Education of the National Council of the Churches of Christ in the United States of America. Used by permission. All rights reserved.

The poem, "Listening Here" by Mark Richardson was used by permission, April 5, 2015.

Series Preface

WE AFFIRM THE VALUE of a Christian liberal arts education. We believe that lifelong development of a Christian worldview makes us more fully human. We attest that engagement in the liberal arts contributes to the process of integrating Christian spirituality with a broad range of disciplinary studies. This integrative process requires that we explore and reflect upon biblical and theological studies while learning effective communication, pursuing healthy relationships, and engaging our diverse global community. We believe that the convergence of academic disciplines opens the door to the good life with enlarged promise for worship of the living God, development of deeper communities, and preparation for service and witness.

Our contributors are dedicated to the integration of faith, life, and learning. We celebrate exposure to God's truth at work in the world not only through preachers, missionaries, and theologians, but also through the likes of poets, artists, musicians, lawyers, physicians, and scientists. We seek to explore issues of faith, increase self-awareness, foster diversity, cultivate societal engagement, explore the natural world, and encourage holistic service and witness. We offer these studies not only as our personal act of worship, but as liturgies to prepare readers for worship and as an opportunity to wrestle with faith and practice through the arts and sciences.

In this series, we proclaim our commitment to interdisciplinary studies. Interdisciplinary studies involves the methodological combination of two or more academic disciplines into one research project. Within a Christian worldview, we address complex questions of faith and life, promote cooperative learning, provide fresh opportunities to ask meaningful questions and address human need. Given our broad approach to interdisciplinary studies, we seek contributors from diverse Christian traditions and disciplines. Possibilities for publication include but are not limited to the following examples: (1) We seek single or multiple author contributions that address Christian faith and life via convergence of two or more academic disciplines; (2) We seek edited volumes that stretch across interdisciplinary lines. Such volumes may be directed specifically at the convergence of two or more disciplines and address a specific topic or serve as a wide-ranging collection of essays across multiple disciplines unified by a single theme; (3) We seek contributors across all Christian traditions and encourage conversations among scholars regarding questions within a specific tradition or across multiple traditions. In so doing we welcome both theoretical and applied perspectives.

The vision for this project emerged among professors at Evangel University (Springfield, MO). Evangel University, owned and operated by the General Council of the Assemblies of God (AG), is the fellowship's national university of arts, sciences, and professions—the first college in the Pentecostal tradition founded as a liberal arts college (1955). Evangel University is a member institution of the Council for Christian Colleges and Universities (CCCU). Consistent with the values and mission of the AG and CCCU, Evangel University exists to educate and equip Christians from any tradition for life and service with particular attention to Pentecostal and Charismatic traditions. Evangel University employs a general education curriculum that includes required interdisciplinary courses for all students. The Evangel University representatives for this series continue to participate in the articulation and development of the Evangel University *ethos* and seek contributors who demonstrate and model confessional integration not only for the Evangel University community and Pentecostals, but for all Christians committed to the integration of faith, learning, and life. We offer this series not only as a gift from the Evangel University community to other Christian communities interested in the intersection of intellectual integration and spiritual and societal transformation, but also as an invitation to walk with us on this journey. Finally, in order to ensure a broad conversation, our editorial committee includes a diverse collection of scholars not only from Evangel University, but also from other traditions, disciplines, and academic institutions that share our vision.

Series Editors

- Paul W. Lewis (Associate Professor of Historical Theology and Missiology at Assemblies of God Theological Seminary)
- Martin William Mittelstadt (Professor of Biblical Studies at Evangel University)

Editorial Board

- Diane Awbrey (Professor of Humanities at Evangel University)
- Jeremy Begbie (Research Professor of Theology at Duke Divinity School)
- Robert Berg (Professor of Theology at Evangel University)
- Jonathan Kvanvig (Distinguished Professor of Philosophy at Baylor University)
- Joy Qualls (Chair & Assistant Professor of Communication Studies at Biola University)
- Brandon Schmidly (Associate Professor of Philosophy at Evangel University)
- Geoffrey W. Sutton (Professor Emeritus of Psychology at Evangel University)
- Grant Wacker (Gilbert T. Rowe Professor of Christian History at Duke Divinity School)
- Michael Wilkinson (Professor of Sociology at Trinity Western University)
- Everett Worthington (Professor of Psychology at Virginia Commonwealth University)

To Leanne, Jenelle, Alyssa, and Zachary Schmidly.
And to Sandra, Nathan, Amy, Julianna, and Amelia Sutton.

Contents

List of Contributors | xi

Acknowledgments | xiii

Part One: Interdisciplinary Foundations of Christian Morality

1 An Introduction to the Foundations of Christian Morality | 3
   By Geoffrey W. Sutton and Brandon Schmidly

2 Philosophical Foundations of Christian Morality | 11
   By Brandon Schmidly

3 Psychological Foundations of Christian Morality | 31
   By Geoffrey W. Sutton

4 Sociological Foundations of Christian Morality | 47
   By Joel Thiessen

5 Jesus, Empire, and Christian Ethics | 62
   Implications for the Moral Critique of Mass Incarceration in the United States
   By Peter Althouse

CONTENTS

Part Two: How Christians Analyze and Respond to Contemporary Moral Issues

6 An Introduction to the Application of Christian Morality | 81
   By Brandon Schmidly and Geoffrey W. Sutton

7 Using Philosophy to Think about Abortion | 87
   By Brandon Schmidly

8 Sexual Minorities, Same-Sex Marriage, and Christian Morality | 103
   By Geoffrey W. Sutton

9 A Woman's Place: Perspectives on Equality | 120
   By Ruth V. Burgess

10 Tensions and Challenges: Christian Morality and Sex Education | 140
   By April Montoya and Shonna Crawford

11 Morality in Local and Global Perspectives | 155
   By Paul W. Lewis

12 Reflections on Christian Morality | 172
   By Geoffrey W. Sutton and Brandon Schmidly

Appendix: Other Morality Topics | 179
   By Geoffrey W. Sutton and Brandon Schmidly

Contributors

Peter Althouse, PhD, Professor of Religion at Southeastern University, Lakeland, FL (PhD University of Toronto).

Ruth V. Burgess, PhD, Emeritus Professor of School of Teacher Education at Missouri State University, Springfield, MO (PhD University of Missouri).

Shonna Crawford, PhD, Professor of Education at Evangel University, Springfield, MO (PhD University of Missouri).

Paul W. Lewis, PhD, Program Coordinator, Intercultural Doctoral Studies at Assemblies of God Theological Seminary, Springfield, MO (PhD Baylor University).

April Montoya, BS, Violence Prevention Advocate, Pueblo Colorado (BS Journalism, Evangel University).

Brandon Schmidly, PhD, Professor of Philosophy at Evangel University, Springfield, MO (PhD University of Missouri).

Geoffrey W. Sutton, PhD Emeritus Professor of Psychology, Evangel University, Springfield, MO (PhD University of Missouri).

Joel Thiessen, PhD, Professor of Sociology, Ambrose University, Calgary (PhD University of Waterloo).

Acknowledgments

WE WISH TO THANK all of the contributors to this volume, without whom this book would not be possible. Without exception they gracefully accepted our feedback.

We are thankful to Martin Mittelstadt and Paul Lewis for including this book in their series. We appreciate Matt Weimer and the staff at Pickwick for recognizing the merit of this book and providing editorial guidance to us throughout the process. We appreciate the comments and endorsement from Joy Qualls.

We thank Evangel University for a financial grant that helped with various expenses associated with completing this project.

We appreciate Beth Barker for her many hours in editing the chapters.

Finally, we wish to express our appreciation to our wives, Sandra Sutton and Leanne Schmidly, for their kindness in affording us the time away from other tasks as we sought to meet our deadlines.

PART ONE

Interdisciplinary Foundations of Christian Morality

1

An Introduction to the Foundations of Christian Morality

Geoffrey W. Sutton

and

Brandon Schmidly

On a Sabbath Jesus was teaching in one of the synagogues, and a woman was there who had been crippled by a spirit for eighteen years. She was bent over and could not straighten up at all. When Jesus saw her, he called her forward and said to her, "Woman, you are set free from your infirmity." Then he put his hands on her, and immediately she straightened up and praised God. Indignant because Jesus had healed on the Sabbath, the synagogue leader said to the people, "There are six days for work. So come and be healed on those days, not on the Sabbath." The Lord answered him, "You hypocrites! Doesn't each of you on the Sabbath untie your ox or donkey from the stall and lead it out to give it water? Then should not this woman, a daughter of Abraham, whom Satan has kept bound for eighteen long years, be set free on the Sabbath day from what bound her?"

Luke 13:10–16 (NIV)

CHAPTER OVERVIEW

WHO WOULD THINK THAT healing somebody would be a bad thing? On the surface, Luke's report indicates Jesus broke a rule about honoring the Sabbath—one of the Ten Commandments. But Jesus used moral reasoning to show how his action was similar to an exception granted by his accusers. In this book, we will attempt to show how Christians can identify or formulate biblical principles of morality.

In response to questions, the apostle Paul provided moral guidance to the first-century churches. Thoughtful Christians continue to seek godly wisdom when confronting contemporary moral situations. The actions they take can affect their own lives and those they love. But Christian leaders can influence the lives of millions when their moral perspectives become the basis for a nation's laws. In this volume, we have assembled a team of contributors to accomplish two primary purposes. In part 1, our authors will offer perspectives on forming an integrated Christian foundation for morality as they draw upon biblical principles and research within their disciplines. In part 2, our authors will demonstrate how to think christianly about contemporary moral matters. Essentially, part 1 provides the bases for Christian moral frameworks and part 2 shows the reader how a Christian moral framework may be applied to moral dilemmas likely to engage Christian communities now and in the next several years.

WHAT IS CHRISTIAN MORALITY?

Before discussing the concept of Christian morality, we want to offer you a working understanding of morality. The subject matter of morality is a normative property. Something is normative if it deals with ideals (norms), and normativity is often expressed with *shoulds* or *oughts*. Morality deals with the normative properties of rightness and wrongness.[1] When someone says *morality*, they may be discussing any number of things related to these properties. They may be discussing the nature of the property, the actions that have that property, the types of people who act according to those properties, or theories, systems, and rules for guiding people according to those properties.

---

1. One should be careful not to confuse being wrong (i.e., immoral) with being wrong (i.e., incorrect) although in some contexts it might mean both.

The terms *morality* and *ethics* are often used interchangeably when discussing these properties. Some scholars insist on a strict distinction between *ethics* and *morality*. But common usage of the terms does not follow any particular distinction. In fact, some contemporary ethics texts explicitly and implicitly use the terms interchangeably.[2] In certain contexts, one term can be more common than the other. For instance, in the context of a discipline of study it is common to hear, "She's studying ethics." It would be strange, though not meaningless, to hear, "She's studying morality." In this volume, we are not concerned with settling a debate over word choice. We desire to produce a clear and easily understandable work on Christian morality. When reading the Bible, it is more common to see the word *immorality* rather than *unethical*. Therefore, we chose to use the words *moral* or *morality* to refer to right and wrong conduct. We encourage our authors to employ common usage as best they can. When some version of *ethics* is more common, we will use it, and the same is true for *moral*. However, when either term is common, we prefer *moral*.

What, then, is Christian morality? In Western cultures, the professions publish codes of ethics that they expect their members to honor. As such, you might hear someone talk about *business ethics*. It so happens that many of the rules of conduct are part of a religion. A theologian or philosopher might write about Christian ethics and refer to broad principles. Many Christians, regardless of profession, look to the Bible as the primary authority regarding matters of right or wrong, we chose to use the phrase *Christian morality* to identify principles about right and wrong conduct that have some basis in Scripture, or are implied by commitments to Scripture.

WHO SHOULD READ THIS BOOK?

1. Students

All of our authors are educators. Most of us have taught students in universities and seminaries. It is natural for us to want to write a book to benefit students. Our aim has been to write primarily for upper-division

---

2. For example, Theroux and Krasemann, *Ethics: Theory and Practice*. In the glossary, the authors state for each term that it is used interchangeably with the other except when "ethics" is referring to the study of morality (e.g., *ethics class*); Shaffer-Landau, *The Fundamentals of Ethics*. The glossary specifies particular phrases (e.g. *moral agent, moral luck, moral exemplar, metaethics, ethical egoism, ethical objectivism*), but it does not specify a distinction between "ethics" and "morality."

undergraduate students, graduate students, and seminary students. We hope you will gain some assistance in forming a foundation for Christian morality and learn ways Christians think about contemporary moral issues. We expect this book will be useful in courses on philosophy, religion, and the behavioral sciences. We hope this will be of equal value to those who identify as Christian as well as to those from other faith traditions or none at all. We anticipate that Christian students will benefit from a better understanding of how their faith might address moral issues. We hope that students who do not identify as Christian will benefit from understanding how thoughtful Christians approach moral matters.

2. Clergy

We wish to engage vocational clergy in the process of forming moral frameworks within their religious traditions and in collaboration with expertise in the behavioral sciences. To this end we have included clergy and Christian scholars among our authors. By including a primary focus on graduate students and seminarians, we hope this book will provide you with a useful review of moral principles as well as new information from the sciences that will broaden your thinking about moral issues beyond the expertise you have gained in your primary discipline.

3. Educated Lay Readers

We anticipate that educated lay readers will find this volume of interest because we have included authors from different academic and career backgrounds who offer multiple perspectives on the moral challenges many Christians face in daily life. We hope you will find that part 1 prepares you to think multidimensionally about the social issues that cause us to ask, "What should we do?" And we hope you find several practical ideas in part 2 that speak to your present situation and prepare you to think morally about situations that might arise in the next several years. Christians from diverse professions interact with others at work and in their communities. They support political agendas and donate to charitable organizations. Each act has the potential to advance or detract from a moral stance.

AN INTRODUCTION TO THE FOUNDATIONS OF CHRISTIAN MORALITY

WHAT WILL YOU FIND IN PART 1?

Chapter 2: Philosophical Foundations of Christian Morality by Brandon Schmidly, Professor of Philosophy at Evangel University.

Brandon Schmidly sets a foundation for Christian morality by providing the philosophical context for discussions of ethics and morality. By providing this foundation, he aims to prepare readers for analyzing and constructing moral arguments. First, he reviews logical principles important to understanding and forming moral arguments. Second, he discusses philosophical claims relevant to objective versus subjective perspectives on morality. Third, he summarizes leading philosophical theories about what is right and wrong.

We expect Christians to refer to Scripture when deciding on a moral course of action. In fact, on major social issues, Christian leaders often create documents that provide moral guidance. For example, Christian leaders have prepared statements on marriage and divorce, abortion, and gambling. The guidance will usually refer to several scriptures and provide reasons why Christians ought to follow a particular course of action. We hope that after reading Schmidly's chapter you are better able to analyze the arguments presented by others as well as think more clearly about what Christians ought to do in a particular situation.

Chapter 3: Psychological Foundations of Christian Morality by Geoffrey W. Sutton, Emeritus Professor of Psychology at Evangel University.

Geoff Sutton aims to explain two major ways that psychological science can help us think about morality. First, he discusses a multidimensional model of human behavior that helps Christians keep in mind that there are internal and external forces that have the potential to influence behavioral actions we judge as moral or immoral. Clues to understanding why people act in certain ways come from recognizing that a person's spiritual state interacts with thoughts, feelings, habitual ways of acting, health, and social factors to influence our moral actions.

In the second part of the chapter he summarizes research conducted by moral psychologists who study how people decide that some conduct is right and some is wrong. He presents a six-dimensional model that will help you analyze the kinds of reasons people offer when justifying moral conduct. You will see that different groups of Christians give greater weight to the six moral dimensions of care, fairness, loyalty, respect for authority, purity, and liberty.

We hope that after considering the complexities of human nature and the actual ways people argue about morality you will be in a better position to discern factors that influence how Christian leaders arrive at different conclusions about a moral course of action. In other words, arriving at a Christian moral judgment is not just about thinking clearly about what to do. Moral judgments are heavily influenced by human nature and many reasons people give for a moral position are influenced by emotion and culture rather than clear thinking from a Christian perspective.

Chapter 4: Sociological Foundations of Christian Morality by Joel Thiessen, Associate Professor of Sociology at Ambrose University.

In this chapter, Joel Thiessen explores four aspects of the relationship between sociology, Christianity, and morality. First, he provides a background for understanding the sociological perspective. Second, he examines different ways sociology and Christianity inform thinking about morality. Third, he considers how a knowledge of sociology can strengthen a Christian response to social issues. Finally, he shows how to think carefully and critically about sociology, Christianity, and morality by examining power and oppression.

We hope that after reading Thiessen's chapter you have a better understanding or the way the values of society influence how Christians think about morality. If we are to think clearly about a Christian approach to a moral issue, we need to be aware of the way the values of our society can influence the moral judgments of all persons, including Christians.

Chapter 5: Theological Foundations of Christian Morality by Peter Althouse, Professor of Religion at Southeastern University.

Peter Althouse provides us with a bridge to the application chapters of part 2 by rooting Christian morality in the dignity of all persons created in the image of God. This God-given dignity is the foundation upon which we affirm that all people have fundamental human rights. Althouse links the notion of Christians as bearers of God's image to Jesus' summary of the law, which mandates love for our neighbors linked to love for God. Christian morality, then, does not just focus on personal conduct but it also requires an active engagement with others in the pursuit of justice for all. Thus grounded in God-given human rights and dignity, Althouse offers us a look at how moral theology will help us discern the application of Christian morality to unjust incarceration practices.

Whether you agree or disagree with Althouse's conclusions, we hope you are able to apply the principles you have learned to analyze his arguments. First, we draw attention to his use of historical context to understand the Bible. His understanding of the context in which Jesus spoke and acted is important to his argument later in the chapter. Second, notice his use of information to support his arguments about the injustice inherent in mass incarceration. Finally, given what Althouse has presented, ask yourself, "What should Christians do?"

BRIEFLY, WHAT WILL YOU FIND IN PART 2?

Our overall purpose in part 2 is to offer examples of how Christian scholars can draw on their faith and insights from their discipline to better understand the moral issues facing contemporary Christians. We asked each scholar to provide examples of how to think about an issue from a Christian perspective. You may agree with some of their ideas, or you may find that you disagree. But whatever you think about the opinions of any particular thinker, we hope you learn how to think more clearly and at a deeper level than ever before. We will provide a more in-depth introduction to part 2 following the chapters in part 1. But for now, we offer a brief summary of the application chapters.

Brandon Schmidly discusses issues of prolife and abortion by explaining the concepts of life and human rights. Geoff Sutton provides an analysis of same-sex relationships, which focuses on maintaining respect for one's own views and those of others. Ruth Burgess provides a learning experience as she invites readers to understand the ongoing struggle of women seeking equality in the workplace and the church. April Montoya and Shonna Crawford examine Christian values in sex education programs. Paul Lewis offers an overview of morality in local and global perspectives. Finally, we editors reflect on the chapters with a focus on integrating what we have learned.

HOW TO READ THIS BOOK

We primarily designed this book to be used as a textbook in introductory courses on ethics and morality. Our second purpose is to offer clergy and lay readers a way to think broadly about social issues from a Christian perspective. We recommend that everyone read the foundational chapters in part 1 because this will give you an introduction to broadly based thinking about morality within a Christian context. Whether taking a course, reading this book as part of a study group, or reading alone, we encourage you to examine the recommended supplementary readings and discuss or write about the questions at the end of each chapter.

Second, we recommend you select several chapters from part 2 so you get a sense of how thoughtful Christians might approach a particular social topic. Again, we encourage you to enhance your experience by referring to the additional readings and answering or discussing the questions.

Geoffrey W. Sutton and Brandon Schmidly
Springfield, Missouri, USA

2

Philosophical Foundations of Christian Morality

Brandon Schmidly

"You shall not hate your brother in your heart, but you shall reason frankly with your neighbor, lest you incur sin because of him."[1]

MANY OF THE MOST influential events of history can be traced back to a human decision. In 1939, Albert Einstein composed a letter to President Roosevelt. In this letter, Einstein described a new process that had the potential to provide a new source of energy. Einstein noted that this new process could possibly be used to build a bomb, and Germany had scientists who were researching it. As a result, Roosevelt made the decision to initiate the Manhattan Project.[2]

In April 1945, President Roosevelt died, and his vice president, Harry Truman, was sworn in as President of the United States. After being briefed on the new bomb, Truman called a committee to study the question of using it against Japan.[3] In July, Truman traveled to Russia to meet with Winston Churchill and Joseph Stalin. While on that trip, Truman toured war-ravaged Berlin. He considered the destruction brought about by Hitler and later wrote, "I fear that machines are ahead of morals by some centuries

1. Lev 19:17 (ESV).
2. Miscamble, *The Most Controversial*, 6.
3. Wainstock, *The Decision*, 52.

and when morals catch up perhaps there'll be no reason for any of it."[4] A few days later, Truman met with Winston Churchill and the chiefs of staff from the United States and Britain. At that meeting, he gave formal consent for using the atomic bomb against Japan.[5]

This series of events highlighted that humanity had reached uncharted capacity for destruction. The question Roosevelt faced ("*Can* we?") is now almost always *yes*. And the question Truman faced ("*Should* we?") is now a much more common and difficult question to answer. The first question is a matter of technology and human ingenuity, the second is a question of morality.

Consider how often you express beliefs about morality. Consider the number of times you use phrases like, "you should . . ." "We ought to . . ." "I have to . . ." "It's ok if they . . ." In addition to these expressions, we often use more robust moral terms like *right*, *wrong*, *duty*, and *guilt*. If we feel strongly, we use terms like *evil*, *honorable*, *obligation*, and *prohibited*. This list is a small sample of the set of moral phrases that we employ on a regular basis. It is a language that reveals our intuitive commitment to moral facts. Some have argued that there is no such thing as morality.[6] However, the vast use of moral language is evidence that we intuitively think moral facts are real. My goal, in this chapter, is to introduce you to philosophy's role in dealing with Christian moral decision-making. I will explain some foundational tools of philosophy, specifically, logical reasoning, moral theories, and meta-ethical claims, and show how they aid the Christian with moral reasoning.

LOGICAL REASONING

Before discussing logical arguments, I would like to briefly discuss the relevance of philosophy in the context of an interdisciplinary book on morality. Morality has two main components, belief and action. It is one thing to have a *belief* about what is morally right. It is often a separate (though certainly related) matter to *behave* morally.

The process of reaching accurate conclusions in any area of study is a philosophical process. In addition, the content of morality is not something

4. Truman and Ferrell, *Off the Record*, 52.

5. Wainstock, *The Decision*, 172–73.

6. For a discussion of the various ways in which this is argued, see Shafer-Landau, *Moral Realism*, 14.

that is easily subject to measurements and observations. Philosophy is the discipline of choice for pursuing conclusions regarding facts about non-physical matters. For both of these reasons, the discipline of philosophy has, rightly, played a prominent role in the field of morality. Creating the atomic bomb was an act of science, determining whether it should be used was an act of ethics.

Though philosophy plays a prominent role, the process of developing right beliefs and translating those beliefs into right behavior is strongly influenced by the human condition. In other words, psychology, physiology, sociology, etc., are fields that provide relevant information regarding morality and affect the accuracy with which we reach conclusions. Furthermore, these fields certainly speak to human behavior. Thus, even given the importance of philosophical foundations for moral thinking, we must remember they are only part of an overall study of ethics.

Many Christians accept (at least implicitly) a view that morality is determined by God's commands in the Bible or prophetic expressions. Ethicists call this view Divine Command Theory, and most contemporary ethicists, even many Christian ethicists, think it is a flawed theory. The main objection is called the Euthyphro Dilemma, and it goes like this.[7]

1. If Divine Command Theory is true, then for any moral act "X," either X is the right thing to do because God commands us to do it, or God commands us to X because it is the right thing to do.

2. If X is the right thing to do because God commands it, then if God had commanded us to torture the innocent, it would be the right thing to do.

3. Surely torturing the innocent could never be the right thing to do.

4. Conclusion 1: So, It is false to say that X is right because God commands it.

5. If God commands us to X because it is the right thing to do, then moral facts are separate from God, and God is subject to them just as we are.

6. Surely God is not subject to anything.

---

7. The title, "Euthyphro Dilemma," gets its name from Plato's dialogue *The Euthyphro*, in which Socrates discusses the nature of piety with religious expert, Euthyphro. Contemporary versions of the Euthyphro Dilemma, such as the one presented here, are not raised by Socrates. However, there are some similarities that account for the name.

7. Conclusion 2: So, It must be false that God commands X because it is the right thing to do.

8. From 4 and 7, it's false that either X is the right thing to do because God commands us to do it, or God commands us to X because it is the right thing to do.

9. So, Divine Command Theory is false.

Many ethicists have been persuaded by this objection. However, some think this objection fails.[8] Unfortunately, explaining the response to this objection would take an entire chapter in itself.[9] A central feature of the response is that God's nature is essentially good, and so the dilemma (in premise 1) is false. But accepting or rejecting Divine Command Theory need not end moral conversations among those who disagree. Christians who accept Divine Command Theory can still discuss morality with those who disagree by appealing to, and arguing for, the aspects of God's nature that ground morality.

Logical arguments can help Christians reach conclusions with confidence. In the following sections we will clarify some of the things that were happening in the argument above and discuss the foundational skill of making good inferences.

MAKING INFERENCES

Reasoning (or logic) is the most important skill in philosophy. It consists in the ability to make good inferences. An inference is the act of starting with known information and figuring out something new. Reasoning is a skill; as such, it can be done well or done poorly. Many failures of moral judgment have come from a lack of good reasoning. This is evidenced by the fact that we often feel like we could have made a better judgment if we had been more thoughtful; or the fact that we are often surprised when what we thought was an implied result of the facts turned out to be wrong. In fact, the process of ethics is often called *moral reasoning*. So, the first philosophical foundation of moral reasoning is skillful thinking (inference-making). In the next few paragraphs, let us briefly look at patterns of reasoning that

---

8. Rachels, *The Elements of Moral Philosophy*, 46–50.
9. For a response, see Adams, *Finite and Infinite Goods*.

are often used in ethics and introduce things that should be considered when evaluating certain reasoning patterns.[10]

The term *deduction* is often used to describe any inference. If you are familiar with Arthur Conan Doyle's writings on Sherlock Holmes, then you will be familiar with this general use of the term. However, deductive inferences are a specific type of inference. Suppose you know that the Tigers and the Bears played in the championship game. Unfortunately, you were unable to watch the game. When you go on social media, you see all of the Bears fans lamenting their team's loss. Even though you have not been told that the Tigers won, you can deductively infer it from two pieces of known information: (1) Either the Tigers or the Bears won. And (2) the Bears did not win. It is so obvious that these two pieces of information imply that the Tigers won that you probably did not put any mental effort into evaluating the inference. However, not all inferences are so obviously valid. And the confidence you have in the conclusions you reach should be a product of the confidence you have in your inferences.

Deductive Inferences[11]

The Tigers-Bears case is an example of a deductive inference. Deductive inferences are those whose conclusions are *guaranteed* by the information (premises). Notice that given the truth of (1) and (2) above, it is *impossible* for the conclusion that the Tigers won to be false. To put it another way, the only way for the conclusion to be false is for either (1) or (2) to be false. In the case of our example, the premises could have been false if either there were other options besides the Tigers winning or the Bears winning (perhaps a team could be replaced), or the Bears didn't lose (you misunderstood the posts on social media). But as long as the premises were true, the conclusion was guaranteed to be true. So the inference from the premises to the conclusion is a good one. We could formalize our inference to look like this: (1) Either A or B. (2) Not B. So, A. Interestingly, we could

---

10. As you read through this chapter and others, look for some of these patterns. In some instances, the pattern is clear. At other times, you will need to reconstruct the argument in order to discover the reasoning pattern.

11 The information in this section and the next is more thoroughly discussed in just about any logic textbook. For instance, see Howard-Snyder, Wasserman, and Howard-Snyder, *The Power of Logic*.

CHRISTIAN MORALITY—PART ONE

substitute anything for the As and Bs in this form, and the premises (if true) would guarantee the conclusion.[12]

Valid deductive inferences are very useful because you can be confident that your conclusion is true, as long as you start with true premises.[13] However, sometimes people think they are making a valid inference when, in fact, it is invalid.[14] For the purposes of this book, I will focus on the most popular valid deductive forms used in moral reasoning: *modus ponens* and *modus tollens*.

Both modus ponens and modus tollens depend on a conditional claim. A conditional claim is a statement of the form, "if A then B." For example, "If you get caught breaking the law, then you will go to jail." Conditional claims can be expressed in a variety of ways; for example, "Given that you get caught breaking the law, you will go to jail." Though the two statements look slightly different, they mean the same thing, and we can reconstruct any conditional claim in the form, "if A then B," and not harm the intent of the original statement.

Let's assume you know that (1) if you get caught breaking the law, then you will go to jail. Furthermore, you overhear someone talking about your friend's antics the night before, and you come to know (2) "my friend got caught breaking the law." You then can know that your friend is (or will be) in jail, and you don't even have to go to the jail in order to know it. This is assuming you *know* (1) and (2). If (1) and (2) are, in fact, true, then it is guaranteed to be true that your friend is in jail. So, the following inference, called modus ponens, is good:

If A then B,
A.
So, B.

---

12. Give it a try. (1) Either the democrats won or the stock market went up. (2) The stock market did not go up. So, the democrats won. Notice that if you deny the conclusion, you must deny one of the premises. And in this case, (1) is obviously questionable. But if you grant (1) and (2) are true, you must grant the conclusion.

13. Here I am using the general term *good* to describe a working deductive form. Philosophers and logicians use the term *valid* to describe any deductive form whose premises guarantee the conclusion. However, many disciplines have a different use for the term *valid* (e.g., when saying that an instrument is valid). So, given the interdisciplinary nature of the book, I will avoid restricting the term *valid* to logic (even though logicians probably used it first!).

14. Bad deductive inferences are formal fallacies. I'll not take the time to discuss common fallacies here.

The second good form, modus tollens, also uses a conditional. Assume again that you know, (1) if you get caught breaking the law, then you will go to jail. Furthermore, while you're drinking your morning coffee, you see your friend walking down the street. So, you now know (2) it is not the case that my friend is in jail. You can now know, despite your concerns about your friend's character, that he did not get caught breaking the law. We can formalize modus tollens to look like this:

If A then B,
Not B.
So, not A.

Modus tollens is a common inference pattern in moral reasoning. Often, to object to a theory, philosophers will produce a hypothetical counter example then reason this way: "If this theory were true, then in my hypothetical example we should get result R. However, R would clearly not be the case. So, your theory must be false."

These argument forms are good precisely as they are presented. Small changes can make the form invalid. Consider the following inference form.

If A then B,
B.
So, A.

Notice, unlike modus ponens, in this instance the argument is asserting B rather than A in premise 2. In this new argument form, the premises do *not* guarantee the conclusion.

Both modus ponens and modus tollens are deductive inference patterns. If you have information that follows the pattern, you can deduce, with 100 percent certainty, the conclusion. Not all good inferences are deductive. There are other inference patterns that are reasonable, even if the information does not *guarantee* the conclusion. These inference patterns are inductive, and they are just as common in moral reasoning.

Probability

While it is nice to have conclusions that are guaranteed, some inferences are reasonable because they are *probable*, that is, the known information makes it likely the new (inferred) belief is true. To quantify it numerically, if your information (premises) implies that a conclusion has a greater than 50 percent probability of being true, then the conclusion is something that should be believed (and your confidence should be proportional to the probability). Suppose you have drawn twenty gumballs, blindly, from a case of gumballs, and nineteen have been red. You now know that (1) nineteen of the last twenty gumballs have been red. It is now most reasonable to believe that the next gumball you draw will be red, even though you have not seen it.[15] It is *possible* that the next gumball will be some color other than red. You even have some evidence for that possibility (one of nineteen). However, the *probability* favors red to the point that it would be *unreasonable* to believe otherwise. Even though this inference is not deductive (i.e., not guaranteed), it is still reasonable. All scientific inferences are inductive, and many moral positions are held on the basis of inductive reasoning.

Reasoning by Analogy

Perhaps the most common inductive reasoning pattern is an analogy. The pattern of an analogy is to have information that two, or more, entities are similar in certain ways and then infer that the entities have an additional similarity. This pattern is especially common in moral reasoning. If you hear someone say, "You can't do that, it would be like . . ." That person is beginning to reason by analogy. We reason by analogy when we consider the parables of Jesus. We reason by analogy whenever we consider a metaphor. Not all analogies are good, and some good analogies are too quickly dismissed. So, in moral decision making, it is important to know how to use and evaluate analogies.

Assume that you have seen the first movie of a popular trilogy, the second of which has just been released in theaters. Your friends are trying to convince you to see the second movie in the theater rather than wait for it to be released online. You, being exceptionally frugal, are only willing to spend the money to see a movie in a theatre if you are highly confident that the experience will be worth the money. Your friends then argue in the

---

15. Not regarding Hume's problem of induction.

following way; the first movie had two main actors, Mr. Heart Throb, and Ms. Bomb Shell. The director of the original was Mr. Bigg Time. For the sequel, the production company was able to re-sign Mr. Throb, Ms. Shell, and Mr. Time. Furthermore, you have made it clear that the first movie is one of your favorite movies of all time, and you wish that you would have seen it in theaters. Your friends now want you to believe that you will love the second movie and you should see it in the theater.

Notice, you currently know the following information: (1) Movies 1 and 2 are similar with regard to the main actors and the director; (2) Movie 1 had the property that you liked it and wanted to see it in the theater. Given this known information, it is supposed to be highly *probable* that you will like Movie 2, even though you know that it is *possible* that you will not. If one were to formalize the pattern of the analogy, it could look like this:

A and B have certain properties in common: P1, P2, P3 . . .
A has another property Px.
So, B has Px.

Unlike deductive inferences, inductive inferences are messy to evaluate, and people can disagree regarding whether the premises make the conclusion probable, even if they agree that the premises are true. In the current example, some individuals may be convinced, with a high degree of confidence, that you will like Movie 2. Someone else may be mildly confident while others may not be convinced at all. If there is such a disagreement, it will likely be because of a specific disagreement regarding one of three considerations. These considerations apply to all analogies and should be evaluated before accepting a conclusion on the basis of an analogy.

First, how relevant are the similarities cited in the premises to the conclusion?[16] There are probably several properties that are irrelevant to the conclusion. Many people like movies on the basis of the actors and director. So, these properties are relevant, and citing these similarities increases the probability that the conclusion will be true. There are likely other similarities that are not relevant. For instance, the titles of both movies contain seven characters, and both movies were distributed by the same

---

16. Even before this consideration, it is relevant to ask whether the premises are true. For instance, are your friends mistaken? Was Bigg Time really the director of Movie 2? Of course, if one of the premises is false, that will weaken the probability created by the argument. However, given that such a consideration should be obvious, I'll focus on other considerations.

distribution company. Even if these similarities are correct, it would be odd for that to be relevant to the conclusion that you will like Movie 2.

If one of your friends disagrees with the conclusion of the original argument, it may be because of a disagreement regarding the relevance of the similarities. Perhaps one friend thinks that you like movies primarily based on the actors while another friend thinks that your movie preferences are based solely on plot (and we don't know if they have a similar plot). Given this disagreement about the relevance of the similarities cited, one may find the conclusion probable while the other does not.

Second, are there any relevant differences between the two things? Even if it is true that they share certain similarities that are relevant, it may be the case that a relevant dissimilarity will completely nullify the probability generated by the similarities. In our movie example, if two friends disagree on whether you will like the movie, perhaps one has the additional information that the movies are of two different genres. While the first was a dramatic thriller, the second movie is a romantic comedy. And because of this difference, there is a disagreement about the probability of the conclusion being true.

Third, are there any other things that have the similar properties, and do they have the property in the conclusion? In our example, perhaps the first movie, by itself, is not enough to persuade you that you will like Movie 2. However, a friend points out that Heart Throb, Bomb Shell, and Bigg Time have worked together on several movies. So she asks you whether you liked each of those movies. If the answer is yes to all, then the inference is strengthened. If the answer is no to all, then the inference is weakened. If there is a combination of yes and no answers, then each would have to be evaluated on the basis of other similarities, differences, and the relevance of each. (Notice how "messy" this can become.)

When considering whether an analogy supports a conclusion, each of these considerations is important to the evaluation of the inference by analogy.[17] If, after considering all of the aspects of the analogy, you find the conclusion is supported by the premises in a highly probable way, you

---

17. These days, people in a disagreement are often too quick to dismiss an analogy without good reason. I often hear people say, "You can't compare X with Y!" and then they move on as if that claim destroys the original argument. Analogous things, by definition, are not identical. There will always be some difference. On the flip side, any two things that exist have something in common (at the very least, that they exist!). So, as long as any similarities are relevant to the conclusion in question, the analogy is worth considering, even if the two entities are drastically different in irrelevant ways.

will have the philosophical support for your conclusion. This support is especially desirable in the domain of ethics.

Now that some basic reasoning principles and patterns have been established, let us employ them to consider some basic claims that are necessary in order to meaningfully engage moral questions.

MORAL OBJECTIVISM

One disagreement that befuddles much of the dialogue in ethics is a disagreement regarding the essential nature of moral claims. Are moral claims objectively true or relative? In this section, I will present some common arguments for rejection of moral relativism, thereby implying that at least some moral claims are objectively true. To say that a claim is objective (or objectively true) is to say that the truth of the claim is in the *object* of the claim. In other words, if it is true that "lying is wrong," we are saying something about lying, *per se*. The truth of an objective claim is independent of what people think. Objectivity is usually contrasted with subjectivity. A claim is subjective if the truth of the claim depends on a person (*subject*). Subjectivism is a type of relativism. A claim is relatively true when the truth of the claim is dependent on how it *relates* to something. There are various types of relativism. When people say that morality is relative, they usually mean that the truth of moral claims depends on how those claims relate to the beliefs and opinions of individuals or groups. And if people change their minds, the truth of the claim could change.

Consider the claim, "Onions taste good." This statement will either be true or false as it relates to the tastes of specific people. It has no truth value on its own. The truth value is not fixed. It may change depending on who utters the sentence. And it may change over time for the same person. When it comes to the claim, "Onions taste good," one can reasonably say, "That may be true for you, but it is not for me." In other words, the truth of the claim is relative.

On the other hand, consider the claim, "There are two cars parked in my driveway right now." The truth of that claim is not relative to any person's beliefs or opinions. Even if all people ceased to exist, this claim would still be either true or false. The truth value of that claim is concrete. If people disagree about that claim, then at least one person is incorrect. It is not reasonable to say, "That may be true for you, but it is not true for me."

Reaching a conclusion on whether moral facts are objective or relative will greatly affect how one engages in the study of ethics. If morality is relative or subjective, then we must focus our study on people and groups of people. If morality is objective, then we must focus on the things that moral claims are about (usually actions).

One way to object to relativism is to undercut the reasons (premises) that people give for accepting it. I'll now consider some of the most common reasons. When one thinks carefully about these common reasons, it will be obvious that none validly (necessarily) imply relativism.

One common reason people give for being relativists is that we have discovered people's moral beliefs vary greatly around the world. While this discovery is true, does this imply moral relativism? If we were to try to make an argument based on this idea, it would have to be something like this:

1. If people's beliefs regarding a matter vary greatly around the world, then the nature of that matter is relative.
2. People's beliefs regarding morality vary greatly around the world.
3. So, the nature of morality is relative.

This pattern is a valid deductive pattern. But when reconstructed this way, it is clear why the inference fails. Premise 1 is false. There are many objective things about which people disagree, whether from person to person or from group to group. At one time, some people thought that smoking caused cancer, but some disagreed. However, it was never the case that it would make sense to say, "That's true for you, but not for me."[18] So, even though it is true that people's beliefs vary, that fact does not imply relativism about morality. With each of the following motivations for relativism, I'll not reconstruct each argument as I did above. I'll leave that for you to do.

A second reason is that people with differing beliefs should be respected and not marginalized. In other words, tolerance has become a value that we should embrace regarding differing cultures' beliefs. Does this imply moral relativism? No. A simple response is that such a view implies tolerance is objectively morally good. Even if we set this response aside, the

---

18. Interestingly, this could be true if some people were biologically constituted such that smoking didn't cause cancer in their bodies, while it did in others. However, this, if true, would still be objectively true. It would be a concrete matter of fact that smoking did cause cancer in some and not in others. The fact would not be subject to people's tastes or beliefs.

objectivist will acknowledge that people who reach different conclusions, or hold to different axioms, may be acting reasonably. People who act in a reasonable manner deserve respect. At one time, there were people who thought the earth was the center of the universe, and they were being as responsible as they could given the available evidence. We now recognize that they were incorrect. However, recognizing that someone is incorrect does not mean that we are disrespecting that person. We may, in fact, be very impressed with the conclusions they reached given their context. That does not imply that the geocentric claim was "true for them but not for us." It wasn't true for either. It is an objective matter.

Third, there are many moral questions such that highly intelligent people have tried to figure out the answer and have not succeeded. In fact, the only thing we know clearly is that we don't know the answer. Again, does this imply that morality is relative? There are smart people investigating the precise age of the universe, and there is not only disagreement, but uncertainty among those who have a considered opinion. That does not mean that, with regard to the age of the universe, one answer may be true for you but not for me.

There are other motivations that we could consider, but these are, I think, the main ones that lead people to be moral relativists, yet these motivations do not actually imply relativism. Undercutting an argument's premises can give you reason to doubt whether the conclusion is true. I will turn now to some positive arguments for the rejection of moral relativism.

First, we need to specify two types of relativism. One is based on individual subjects (*subjectivism*). And one is based on groups (let's call it *conventionalism*).[19] If relativism is true, then it is likely true in at least one of these two forms.

First, consider conventionalism. If the truth of morality is a matter of the views of groups, then, by definition, when people act against the views of the relevant group, they are acting immorally. This view has some practical problems. We are each members of several groups. I'm a member of my family, my town, my church, my state, my nation, the Society of Christian Philosophers, a university faculty, etc. Clearly some of these groups have conflicting moral positions, and that creates, at least, a practical problem.[20] Unless there is an objective way to determine which group is the real moral authority, conventionalism will likely reduce to subjectivism because it will

19. Following the nomenclature of Pojman, "A Defense."
20. Ibid.

be up to me to determine which group is the right group. I will address subjectivism below.

However, let's set aside the practical problem of many groups and deal with the nature of conventionalism. Consider the number of famous people who have gone against the conventions of his or her society: Mahatma Gandhi, Martin Luther, Martin Luther King Jr., and even Jesus. These people are, supposedly, moral stalwarts. In fact, their morality consisted, in part, in their willingness to counter the conventions of their society. Let's set up this argument as a modus tollens:

1. If conventionalism is true, then Mahatma Gandhi, Martin Luther, Martin Luther King Jr., and Jesus were immoral (by definition).[21]

2. It is not the case that Mahatma Gandhi, Martin Luther, and Martin Luther King Jr., and Jesus were immoral.

3. So, it is not the case that conventionalism is true.[22]

Since this is a deductive inference, if the premises are true, the conclusion is guaranteed to be true. It is not a matter of probability. So, to deny the conclusion requires one to deny one of the premises. The first premise seems to be a clear implication of conventionalism. Someone could object by noting that, while our band of moral stalwarts acted contrary to their society, they were acting consistently with the views of another group. Granting this will, however, only push the problem back a step. For any group, there will be members of the group that will act contrary to the group as a matter of moral principle. In that instance, the member will be immoral by definition if conventionalism is true. The only way to avoid this is to have a group that is morally infallible. However, their moral infallibility will have to be an objective fact which, in turn, would make morality objective.

The second option is to deny premise 2 and say that the band of moral stalwarts were, in fact, immoral. I take it that the failure of such objection is too obvious to merit discussion. If anyone is committed to conventionalism to the point that he or she is willing to accept the implication that our band of moral stalwarts were, in fact, immoral, then that will have to be the point at which we disagree.

---

21. To make the argument fully explicit, we could first say: (1) if Conventionalism is true, then acting contrary to the moral conventions of one's society is, by definition immoral. And (2) Gandhi, Martin Luther, and Martin Luther King Jr. acted contrary to the moral conventions of their societies.

22. Pojman, "A Defense," 48.

I'll turn now to subjectivism. The view that moral truths are based on individual beliefs. If subjectivism is true, then, by definition, being moral is a matter of doing what one sincerely believes. However, if we consider what we intuitively mean when we talk about morality, we realize that we are often referencing something other than just our sincere beliefs. Let's reconstruct this argument as well:

1. If subjectivism is true, then everyone's sincere beliefs about morality are never incorrect.
2. It is not the case that everyone's sincere beliefs about morality are never incorrect.
3. So, it is not the case that subjectivism is true.

The most controversial premise is premise 2. However, denying premise 2 has some unintuitive implications. If you deny premise 2, then you must accept that no one who is sincere is ever mistaken when he or she thinks an act is moral. People *could* act immorally, but only if they act contrary to their sincere beliefs. As long as they act with sincerity, they are never immoral and never in error. This is surely false.

In this section we set out to advance the claim that morality is essentially objective and not essentially relative. In the process, we demonstrated how to employ philosophical rigor when investigating foundational claims about morality. We first considered the fact that the most common motivations for relativism do not actually imply a denial of objectivism, then we considered and defended arguments for the falsehood of conventionalism and subjectivism. As a result, we should move forward in our study of ethics with an understanding that we are not merely talking about people's tastes. We are investigating a domain with real facts.[23] Morality is not such that the essential facts are "true for you but not for me." People and cultures (including our own) can be sincere about their moral beliefs and yet be incorrect. The recognition of the possibility of error does not imply disrespect for such people or cultures. Furthermore, we can say that those who show disrespect for sincere people and cultures are objectively morally wrong.

---

23. We have not addressed the question of moral realism. It is possible to be a moral objectivist and yet an anti-realist. That is, you can agree that moral facts, if they exist, are objective and deny that any exist. There are good arguments against this view. See Shafer-Landau, *Moral Realism*. I will not include them in our discussion here since most readers of this text will come with the intuitive belief that there are real moral facts.

MORAL THEORY: THE MEANING OF RIGHT AND WRONG

Having determined that morality is essentially an objective domain, I'll turn to the prevailing comprehensive theories of morality. Just as we advance comprehensive theories of the physical world (Newtonian physics, Einstein's Relativity, et al.) in order to better answer particular questions in areas such as medicine or electronics, we can investigate comprehensive theories of morality in order to better answer particular moral questions about abortion or human sexuality.

Utilitarianism

Perhaps the most initially intuitive comprehensive moral theory is Utilitarianism. Utilitarianism is most often associated with philosophers John Stuart Mill and Jeremy Bentham. Utilitarianism is a consequentialist theory. A consequentialist theory is any theory that appeals to consequences to determine moral rightness. The idea of consequentialism is captured in the phrase, "The ends justify the means." To put it more precisely, the ends, or consequences, determine the moral status of an action. The particular consequence that Utilitarianism appeals to is pleasure.

According to Utilitarianism, the moral rightness of an action is determined by the amount of pleasure over pain the act produces. For example, suppose you are deciding whether to lie to the Nazis about people hidden in your house. All you need to do is calculate the pleasure over pain that will be produced by each possible action, lying or telling the truth. It is clear that telling the truth would result in the pain, suffering, and death of the people in your house with little pleasure produced for the Nazis. And lying would result in great pleasure for the people and their families and little pain for the Nazis. So, lying will produce the most pleasure over pain, and, according to Utilitarianism, the right act is to lie to the Nazis.[24]

However, let's consider a famous response from Philippa Foot against Utilitarianism. It begins with a hypothetical case. Suppose you are a surgeon. You have a patient come into your clinic who is completely healthy. It just so happens that you have five other patients in the clinic, each of whom will die if they don't receive an organ transplant today, each requiring a

---

24. Specifically what *makes* it right is its producing the greatest amount of pleasure over pain. It isn't just that pleasure is an indicator, it is the rightness-maker.

different organ. After doing some questioning, you realize that the healthy patient is a perfect match for all five and has organs sufficient to save all five. You also discover that the healthy man has no family, no friends, and does not lead a happy life. After doing a pleasure-pain calculation, it is clear that the most pleasure will be produced by harvesting the healthy man's organs and saving the other five. So, according to Utilitarianism, you should harvest the organs of the healthy man. However, it is intuitively clear that it is grossly immoral to do such a thing. As a result, Utilitarianism must be, to some extent, false.[25]

What best explains the morality of the organ harvesting case is the fact that the healthy man has rights that should be respected, regardless of the pleasure or pain that results from respecting those rights.

RIGHTS AND DUTIES

Contemporary western culture has largely adopted the term *rights* as a way to discuss morality. We see that terminology expressed in the Declaration of Independence. A rights-based theory offers the most plausible explanation in the organ-harvesting case. Rights are moral properties, or protections, that reside in objects (people) or actions regardless of the consequences. So, if a person has a right to life, there is something about the person such that it is *prima facie* immoral to kill him, even if you could save five others.

Rights-based moral theories are often associated with philosophers John Locke and Immanuel Kant. The concepts that are associated with rights can help us make sense of discussing morality for most cases. As was mentioned earlier, a right is a moral protection. With every right, there is a corresponding duty that at least one other person has. For instance, your right to life creates a duty on the part of everyone else. The *prima facie* duty is that they not kill you. If I were your boss and you did an agreed upon job, you have a right to compensation, and I have a duty to compensate. Rights-based theories often work well within a Christian belief system. This is because, as creator, God is the ultimate right-holder over everything. Rights had by created beings are delegated to them from God. John Locke offers an account of how all authority comes from God.[26]

A practical difficulty with reaching moral conclusions within a rights-based framework is produced by the fact that rights can conflict. Often,

---

25. Foot, "The Problem of Abortion."
26. Simmons, *The Lockean Theory*, 26–36.

moral dilemmas are cases of conflicting rights, and it can be difficult to assess which rights are stronger than others. For instance, suppose you promised your friends that you would meet them for dinner, and you promised your boss that you would attend an after-hours seminar. By mistake, you did not realize that both were at the same time, and you do not have any way to contact either your friends or your boss to be released from a promise. In this instance, the simple fact that you have a duty and both your friends and your boss have a right against you does not make it clear what the moral course of action would be. No matter what you do, you will break a promise. In cases such as this, the difficult analysis of weighing one right against another is how one must reach a moral conclusion in a rights-based system.

Even in spite of the messy analysis, there are some cases where a rights-based theory does not get the correct answer. For instance, suppose that it is discovered that I am a carrier of an incurable disease. Unless I am killed, there is a high probability that I will infect others and bring about an epidemic that will destroy mankind. Suppose, in this case, I was not responsible for acquiring the disease, and I will not give consent to anyone to kill me. Intuitively, it seems like saving the lives of others is more important than not killing me (a conclusion supported by Utilitarianism). A rights-based view of morality would seem to conclude that it is wrong to kill me in this instance. This dilemma demonstrates that, at times, both rights and consequences figure into a moral evaluation.

While these theories are the most widely adopted moral theories, there are others which base morality on properties such as self-interest, motive, and virtue. While each of these brings relevant considerations to the topic of moral reasoning, it would take too much space to discuss each in this chapter.

SUMMARY

In this chapter, I have reviewed the philosophical foundations that are important for Christians involved in moral reasoning. The discipline of philosophy deals with the search for moral truths, and it is the domain where moral theories are developed in order to more accurately determine when an action is moral. I introduced the important skill of inference-making and reviewed several argument patterns for making sound and cogent inferences. I then demonstrated this skill in the process of reaching an important philosophical conclusion about the nature of morality, namely, that it is a matter of objectivity. Finally, I reviewed two of the major theories of morality, which provide a framework for reaching moral conclusions.

While philosophy helps with reaching conclusions about morality, morality is also a matter of behavior, our interaction with others, and our relationship with God. As such, the following foundational chapters from psychology, sociology, and theology are necessary for a well-developed understanding for Christian moral decision-making.

ADDITIONAL RESOURCES

1. Regarding rights, there are often cases in the news about the right to die. There is disagreement about whether such a right exists (a moral right, not necessarily a legal right). The state of Oregon has passed legislation regarding this matter. https://public.health.oregon.gov/ProviderPartnerResources/Evaluationresearch/deathwithdignityact/Pages/index.aspx.

2. Do we have a duty to be altruistic, or is altruism's moral worth best explained by Utilitarianism? Peter Singer discusses this issue. http://on.wsj.com/1BWMTPB.

3. Whistleblowers often face a dilemma of conflicting duties. The US Department of Labor has recently issued a protection program for whistleblowing. http://www.whistleblowers.gov/.

DISCUSSION QUESTIONS

1. Take a current moral issue and defend a position by using an analogy. Go through the steps of evaluating an analogy to evaluate your defense. After evaluation, do you still think it is a good defense? What might someone say who disagrees with your conclusion?

2. Many people in society, including Christians, are relativists about morality. What do you think motivates most people's relativism? Can you produce a successful argument based on that idea?

3. Is John Locke correct that rights come from God? If so, is it possible for an atheist to be moral? If so, how would an atheist explain morality?

4. Considering the example above, should a person be killed if they carry an incurable disease and there is the risk of destroying humanity? How do you account for your answer? Is this example relevantly similar to a case where the NSA violates someone's rights for the protection of US citizens? Are you appealing to rights? Utility? Or something else in your answer?

REFERENCES

Adams, Robert Merrihew. *Finite and Infinite Goods: A Framework for Ethics*. Oxford: Oxford University Press, 1999.

Bentham, Jeremy. *An Introduction to the Principles of Morals and Legislation*. Gloucestershire, UK: Clarendon, 1879.

Foot, Philippa. "The Problem of Abortion and the Doctrine of Double Effect." *Oxford Review* 5 (1967).

Howard-Snyder, Frances, Ryan Wasserman, and Daniel Howard-Snyder. *The Power of Logic*. 5th ed. Columbus, OH: McGraw-Hill, 2012.

Kant, Immanuel. *Groundwork for the Metaphysics of Morals*. Edited by Thomas E. Hill Jr. Translated by Arnulf Zweig. Oxford: Oxford University Press, 2002.

Mill, John Stuart. *Utilitarianism*. Peterborough, ON: Broadview, 2010.

Miscamble, Wilson D. *The Most Controversial Decision: Truman, the Atomic Bombs, and the Defeat of Japan*. Cambridge: Cambridge University Press, 2011.

Pojman, Louis P. "A Defense of Ethical Objectivism." In *Life and Death: a Reader in Moral Problems*, edited by Louis P. Pojman, 43–54. Boston: Wadsworth, 2000.

Rachels, James. *The Elements of Moral Philosophy*. 2nd ed. Columbus, OH: McGraw-Hill, 1993.

Shafer-Landau, Russ. *Moral Realism: A Defence*. Oxford: Oxford University Press, 2003.

Simmons, A. John. *The Lockean Theory of Rights*. Princeton: Princeton University Press, 1992.

Truman, Harry S., and Robert H. Ferrell. *Off the Record: The Private Papers of Harry S. Truman*. Columbia, MO: University of Missouri Press, 1997.

Wainstock, Dennis D. *The Decision to Drop the Atomic Bomb: Hiroshima and Nagasaki: August 1945*. New York: Enigma, 2013.

3

Psychological Foundations of Christian Morality

Geoffrey W. Sutton

I do not understand what I do. For what I want to do I do not do, but what I hate I do.

—The Apostle Paul[1]

HAVE YOU EVER FELT so tired that all you wanted to do was sleep? How long do you think you could go without sleep? In 2014, the U.S. Senate released a report of the CIA's program on interrogation and detention programs. People were captured and subjected to psychological and bodily pain in an effort to extract information that might lead to the capture of terrorists, foil plots to kill Americans, or stop plans to destroy U.S. interests. Prisoners were denied sleep for as much as one hundred and eighty hours. Prisoners were beaten, stripped, frozen, and subjected to water boarding. U.S. personnel even threatened to cut the throat of a prisoner's mother.[2]

U.S. Senator John McCain declared, "This question isn't about our enemies; it's about us. It's about who we were, who we are, and who we aspire to be. It's about how we represent ourselves to the world."[3] The story

---

1. Rom 7:15 (NIV).
2. Senate Select Committee, 2014.
3. Horsey, "John McCain Has Moral Clarity."

illustrates several points about morality, psychology, and Christianity. Here is a partial list of questions we can raise.

1. Is torture moral? That is, is it right or wrong? Under what conditions, if any, would it be a morally right thing to do to harm another person?
2. Most members of the U.S. Congress identify as Christian. When Christians go to work, should they draw on their faith to make moral decisions? If so, is the torture of captured persons consistent with Christian morality?
3. Are there qualities about people like Senator McCain or nations that give them the *right to speak* about moral issues?

Groups, organizations, and nations have often acted to harm other people. Usually, an official group like an intelligence agency will offer reasons for the harm and establish guidelines on what can and cannot be done. For example, a nation might permit beatings and threats to extract information from a terrorist they hope will prevent the bombing of a hospital. Psychologists find that when it comes to moral judgments, harming others is one of the primary things people consider wrong. And concerns about harm are consistent with at least a superficial reading of Jesus' teaching about loving our neighbors as ourselves and doing good to our enemies. Another contribution from psychological research is the consistent finding that information obtained during torture is unreliable.

The story also illustrates two other dimensions of moral psychology—loyalty and respect for authority. Some people blasted the senators responsible for making the report public as being disloyal to the United States. But when Senator McCain spoke out against the actions of the CIA, he was accorded a measure of moral authority.[4] He had earned the authority to speak—not because he was an elected leader—but because he had been subject to torture as a U.S. soldier who had been a Prisoner of War. Notice that in the cases of loyalty and respect for authority, there is no particular logic as to why we ought to be loyal or respect some people more than others. But we value loyalty and respect as ways people ought to act.

4 Ibid.

INTRODUCTION

Human beings have a sense of right and wrong. Before children can articulate moral principles, they know when they have lied, taken something that did not belong to them, or disobeyed a parent. Christians obviously learn more about righteousness or right living from the Bible. Jesus' summary of the Old Testament law is well known—love God and love your neighbor.[5] But people face situations not explicitly addressed in the Bible. Thoughtful Christians wonder about lying to protect others, ignoring the wrongdoing of others, how much they should sacrifice to help people in need, what are right actions toward the environment, and when artistic expression is merely pornography. Thinking people concerned about doing the right thing take time to ask, "What should I do?" Psychological scientists identify the factors that influence peoples' moral decisions and how people come to different conclusions about what is right and wrong.

My purpose in this chapter is to explain two major ways that psychological science can help us think about morality. First, I will introduce you to a multidimensional model of human behavior that will help us keep in mind that there are internal and external forces that have the potential to influence our behavior. Perhaps you have expressed some wonderment like the Apostle Paul at why it is that we may do something we really do not want to do. Some clues to understanding our struggle can come from recognizing that our Christian spirituality interacts with our thoughts, feelings, habitual ways of acting, health, and social factors to influence our moral conduct.

In the second part of this chapter, I will summarize research conducted by moral psychologists interested in learning how people appraise some conduct as right and some as wrong. Specifically, I will introduce you to a six-dimensional model that will help you analyze the kinds of reasons people offer when justifying moral conduct. The six dimensions draw upon the extensive work by Jonathan Haidt and his colleagues.[6] This model will help us understand how different Christians can judge the same conduct as moral or immoral—right or wrong. It often turns out that different groups of Christians give greater weight to the six moral dimensions of care, fairness, loyalty, respect for authority, purity, and liberty.

---

5. Luke 10:27.
6. For a summary, see Haidt, *The Righteous Mind*, 128–54.

CHRISTIAN MORALITY—PART ONE

WHY DO PEOPLE DO WHAT THEY DO NOT WANT TO DO?

You have probably heard the expression, "gun to the head." The phrase conjures up images of an action movie in which someone is forced at gun point to say or do something they do not want to do in order to save their life or the life of a loved one. Fortunately, most life situations fall far short of such poignant moments. In most situations we act morally based on the way we have been raised and guided by the people in our community. But from time to time we face genuine moral dilemmas—occasions when we are not sure what we ought to do. In some cases, we look back on something we did and wonder, "Why on earth did I do something like that?" In this section, I take a look at six factors that interact to influence how we act. The six factors can be remembered by using the acronym *SCOPES*: Spiritual, Cognitive (thinking), Observable behavior, Physical/biological, Emotional, and Social context. Each of these six factors can be thought of as a source of influence.[7]

1. Spirituality

Many people, including psychological scientists, view spirituality as a core factor in human functioning. Although people vary in the degree to which they commit to any faith, about 80 percent of the world's population reports a religious affiliation. And a substantial percentage of those (31 percent) are Christians.[8] By reading the Bible, participating in church education programs, and observing Christian role models, Christians learn about right and wrong. Psychologists refer to beliefs and other thoughts as cognitions. Cognitions can also include mental images such as dreams. Spirituality is more than a set of beliefs and images. Christians also behave in ways considered spiritual or religious. They pray, donate funds, study the Bible, help others, and do many other things. A spiritual faith informs life goals and the behavior that leads to reaching those goals. Some of our actions may be considered moral acts as in helping others or speaking out against immorality. Spirituality also influences our feelings. People may feel uplifted and hopeful when participating in worship. They may also feel guilty when they realize some course of action violated their beliefs or offended God.

---

7. For a recent application of the SCOPES model, see Sutton and Mittelstadt, *Loving God*, 157–66.

8. Pew Research Center, *Global Religious Landscape*, 9.

Moreover, spirituality influences our experiences such that any context can become spiritual. We can expect church to be a spiritual context. Going to church on a Sunday morning carries a set of expectations about how to behave. The greetings, songs, art, and architecture can influence our experience even when we may not have felt very *spiritual* that morning. In contrast, people report meaningful moments when driving or taking a walk. Spirituality is pervasive. Because spirituality is a substantial part of human nature, it is important to understand the link between a person's spirituality and their moral conduct.

Evidence of this link comes from a recent study of judges. We expect judges to be knowledgeable of the law and impartial in their judgments. Researchers Brian Bornstein and Monica Miller found that Catholic and Baptist judges in the U.S. were more supportive of religion than other Christian and non-Christian judges. Not surprisingly, Evangelical Christian judges were the most conservative on issues of gender discrimination and obscenity.[9] The research on judges suggests that Christians will be influenced by their faith when making moral decisions.

2. Cognition

Every year, millions of people set goals to change some aspect of their behavior. Some want to lose weight, others vow to control their anger, and others intend to spend more time reading their Bibles or praying. Like the Apostle Paul, many find their behavior does not match their goals. They do not do what they wish to do. Research summarized by Daniel Kahneman helps explain the discrepancy.[10] Human beings function as if they had two minds.

For the most part, we perform our daily activities in a type of automatic mode. We are so used to a morning routine that we do not have to think much about it, which sometimes results in funny outcomes, like mismatched clothes and shoes. Many have had the experience of driving a familiar route and forgetting to stop somewhere as if they were driving on autopilot. Not only do we breathe and regulate our hearts automatically, but our brains can also guide us into performing a significant number of other routines. Some of these routines are complex, like responding to common conversation topics or making quick judgments on moral matters. For the

---

9. Bornstein and Miller, "Does a Judge's Religion," 112–15.
10. Kahneman, *Thinking, Fast and Slow*, 20–24.

most part, we think, feel, and act quickly in response to life events. People in the habit of performing morally right actions do not need to think about telling the truth, refraining from theft, or many other common acts judged right and wrong.

We all experience problems in life, which cause us to pause and think. This type of thinking requires effort. To solve problems we must perform a number of actions including gathering information, weighing the reliability of the information, and trying to figure out how the information we have will help us make the right choice. Some of these decisions involve moral matters. It turns out that effortful thinking does not come easily. Humans avoid hard work. Students and employees procrastinate and seek to avoid difficult projects. Decisions that require careful analysis or stopping an easy course of action are quickly overridden by fast, action-oriented habits. When faced with a choice to skip a party where most will use illegal drugs, ignore an opportunity to cheat on an exam, or resist cheating in a relationship, people are at risk of acting on auto-pilot, which will depend on their usual thought-action sequences. And if they are not in the habit of acting morally, they are not likely to interrupt their thinking to ponder the potential negative consequences that might help them avoid an immoral act.

In addition to the cognitive factor of avoiding effortful thinking, another cognitive factor is worth mentioning because of its relevance to moral decisions. There are significant problems with human memory. In fact, the problems are so well known that eyewitnesses become a problem in court because they often give contradictory information. They contradict themselves and the statements by other eyewitnesses. The temptation is to think someone is lying and we just need to dig deeper to find the truth. Of course, it may be true that a witness is lying. But researchers have found repeatedly that human memory is dynamic and not fixed. What we remember about an event changes over time. We miss details, which are often important in moral judgments about a criminal act. And when people ask questions of eyewitnesses, the witnesses remember facts differently. Eyewitnesses can sincerely add information that was not present as well as omit important details.[11] A good example of how faulty cognition can result in moral harm is the case of Ronald Cotton.[12] Jennifer Thompson was raped and mistakenly identified Ronald Cotton from a police lineup. She was sure she selected her rapist. Cotton was convicted and spent years in prison for a

---

11. For a summary, see Loftus and Ketcham, *Witness for the Defense*, 14–30.
12. See Thompson-Cannino, *Picking Cotton*.

crime he did not commit. Eventually, Cotton was freed when the real rapist was discovered.

3. Observable Behavior

In contrast to thoughts, feelings, and biological events that happen within us, our behaviors are observable and thus open to be judged as moral or immoral. Although psychologists do not agree on which behavior patterns are close to universal, many find five patterns to have wide applicability. These five patterns are known as personality traits and are sometimes called the Big Five. The word *OCEAN* is an acronym for the five traits of Openness, Conscientiousness, Extroversion, Agreeableness, and Neuroticism.

Research is needed to better link these five traits to moral actions, but a look at the behavior patterns associated with these five can help us understand a person's tendency to behave in ways considered moral or immoral. People high in openness are prone to consider many ideas including different opinions as to what is right and wrong. At the other end of the spectrum are those who are closed to considering alternative opinions of morality.

Conscientiousness is an obvious moral virtue. People high in conscientiousness are reliable and follow the rules, in contrast to those low on this trait. Extroversion is contrasted with introversion and is not directly tied to a moral virtue, yet because we know that people enjoy social contact and approval, we may suspect that those high on extroversion would be more inclined to go along with a group than those who are highly introverted. In this instance, the moral actions of the group may have a strong influence for good or bad on people who highly desire the approval of the group. Agreeableness is a desirable trait in friends and employees. Yet the downside can be seen in those who are so agreeable that they find it hard to resist the demands of leaders to violate moral rules. Finally, neuroticism refers to the dysregulation of emotions in contrast to those who present as emotionally stable. Emotions help motivate behavior. Those prone to anger and related destructive behavior will find it more difficult than others to act morally when threatened or placed under stress.

4. Physiology

Our biological state influences our moral actions. Hungry people aggressively seek food and will steal to satisfy their needs. In one study, judges granted more favorable judgments early in the morning and just after a break.[13] Snacks influence brain glucose levels, which is important to effortful thinking.

Our brains vary in their capacity for self-control. The capacity for self-control is important to holding people morally accountable for their actions. People with diseases like Alzheimer's gradually lose control over their actions. Some people who experience forms of brain damage in which self-control centers are damaged also lose self-control. The loss of biologically based self-control can result in actions usually considered immoral. In addition, people vary in their self-control over sexual activity. A small percentage of people are asexual and have no interest in sexuality. A small percentage of persons experience a very high sex-drive. The level of the hormone testosterone is a significant factor in sexual expression.[14] When people with a high sex-drive also have lower brain-based inhibitions, they find it very difficult to control sexual urges compared to people with an average sex drive and a normally functioning inhibition mechanism.

5. Emotions

Positive and negative feelings accompany moral judgments. People feel passionately about many social issues, and feelings can motivate people to behave in ways judged moral or immoral. Anger can interfere with making a persuasive moral argument, and anger can motivate aggressive acts resulting in harm to people and property. On the positive side, those high in empathy are more forgiving and compassionate. Although love is more than an emotion, it certainly includes powerfully strong feelings. Some people who have strong feelings of loving God also appear motivated to love others.[15]

6. Social Context

Social context includes locations, time frames, and the people present in our social environments. Pastors notice that many people censure their language and jokes when they become aware of their presence. Over the

---

13. Danziger et al., "Extraneous Factors," 6889–92.
14. Bancroft, "Sexual Desire," 166–71.
15. Wilkinson and Althouse, *Catch the Fire*, 45–69.

years, I have heard many sermons by pastors encouraging people to live the Christian life the rest of the week, which highlights the common observation that people behave well in church on Sundays but seem less aware of what God expects the rest of the week.

Researchers have found that the simple placement of an image of a pair of eyes by a money box in a break room increases the payment for snacks compared to conditions when the eyes were not present.[16] It seems the idea of being watched helps regulate moral behavior. Although we often view moral behavior as an individual choice, research indicates our choices are influenced by people and things within our environment and we may not always be aware of subtle influences that nudge us toward a moral or immoral action.

HOW DO SINCERE PEOPLE REACH DIFFERENT CONCLUSIONS ABOUT RIGHT AND WRONG?

I now turn to consider a different perspective on morality. In the first section, I looked at six sources of influence on moral actions. In this section, I examine the justifications people give for a particular moral outcome. A great deal of the information was summarized in a 2012 book, *The Righteous Mind*, by Jonathan Haidt and his colleagues. When asked about why a particular course of action is right or wrong, people give reasons. Those reasons tend to fall in one of six categories, which can be viewed as six dimensions that create a strong basis for one moral position or another. It turns out that many people are polarized into groups as either progressive (sometimes called liberal) or conservative. Conservatives tend to give answers that span the range of the six dimensions, but liberals tend to emphasize the two dimensions of care/harm and fairness/justice. Sometimes progressive Christians also express concerns for a third dimension of liberty in contrast to oppression.

1. Care vs. Harm

Jesus' story about the Good Samaritan offers a contrast between a person who cared and those who did not care for a man who had been robbed,

---

16. Bateson et al., "Cues of Being Watched," 412–14.

beaten, and left on a roadside.[17] Both conservative and progressive Christians encourage caring and speak against harming others. We could expect both conservatives and progressives to follow the example of the Good Samaritan in caring for a person who had been victimized. The difference between conservative and progressive groups is often one of emphasis. For progressive Christians, caring is one of two major emphases (the other is fairness) when it comes to evaluating the morality of a course of action. Conservatives will draw upon five or six dimensions when making judgments. It is easy to see why Christians can condemn drunkenness, child abuse, trafficking, and many other actions as immoral because of the harm done. A difference can be seen in the different responses of Christians toward same-sex marriage. Although conservatives can recognize the harm done when a person is deprived of the happiness that comes from marriage, conservatives also worry about the harm done to their community if Christians are led to believe such a lifestyle is acceptable. In contrast, progressive Christians focus heavily on the harm done to the people expected to deny their sexuality for the rest of their lives.

2. Fairness

The idea that all people should be treated the same arises early in development when children learn to play games according to the rules. Anger arises in children and adults when some people get away with breaking the rules. Fairness implies equal treatment and is the cry of groups that have advocated that people should not be discriminated against based on their age, biological sex, skin color, or religious affiliation. Fairness is of high importance to progressive Christians who often support social justice issues. In recent years, fairness and equality emphases were part of the basis for arguing that laws preventing same-sex couples from marrying were unjust and therefore immoral. Conservative Christians recognized the inequality but drew upon other moral dimensions to emphasize considerations such as respect for the authority of scriptural teachings supporting marriage as between one man and one woman. The respect for Scripture overlapped with a concern for loyalty to the traditional teachings of the church compared to a perceived arrogance in thinking hundreds of years of church teaching was suddenly wrong.

17. Luke 10:25–37.

3. Liberty vs. Oppression

Liberty is akin to a battle cry for U.S. Christians. The U.S. was founded on a call for liberty and freedom from the perceived oppressive rule of King George III of Great Britain. Christians are called to consider the oppressed. Jews and Christians are reminded about the oppression of the Israelites in Egypt and the liberation from slavery led by Moses. Although contemporary Christians reject slavery as immoral, this was not the case throughout most of history. The abolition of the African slave trade took place over many years. Many Christians held slaves and supported slavery. Even after the U.S. officially ended slavery in the mid-1800s, it was a century before laws limiting the freedom of African Americans would be overturned. Black Americans were not welcomed in white churches. To this day, many churches remain unofficially segregated.[18] The liberation of women from restrictive policies is another example of a group of people who have been oppressed. Here are three common examples of the way progressive Christians emphasize the first three dimensions: African Americans and women have been *harmed* by the effects of restrictive laws, treated as *unequal* to white men or men in general, and deprived of certain *freedoms*. Although many conservatives would also agree to the forgoing three examples, many conservatives will also express some of the following three additional considerations.

4. Loyalty vs. Betrayal

Loyalty is a virtue. Countries expect their citizens to be loyal and to support their fellow citizens when under attack. Betraying one's country is treason and can be punished by death. Employers expect loyalty from their employees. Disloyalty can result in loss of employment or restrictions on being promoted. If you are a member of a particular church, you are expected to support the beliefs of your church and support the needs of fellow believers through prayer and donations. Jesus expected loyalty from his followers. The betrayal of Jesus by Judas is a classic example of disloyalty in the Bible. Parents expect their children to be loyal to their family. In extreme cases, disloyal children are disinherited by their parents. Loyalty binds people together in fellowship and promotes survival when a group is threatened as in times of war. The downside of loyalty is the support of immorality. Even

---

18. Lipka, "Many U.S. Congregations."

people who would not actively promote slavery or discrimination against a minority group have a hard time speaking out against their leaders for fear of being considered disloyal or a traitor and because of a strong bond of loyalty toward those who have provided for one's welfare. Speaking against one's government or church leadership carries risks.

5. Respect for Authority vs. Disobedience

Respect for authority is a common virtue in most groups. Children and young persons are expected to respect their elders. Christians are expected to respect the church leaders as people chosen by God to lead the faithful. All are expected to respect God by following the teachings of the Bible. Throughout the centuries of Christian history, leaders have risen to challenge the authority of church leaders. Some paid with their lives. Others were removed from fellowship. Many Christian groups are formed by leaders who broke away from the authority of a leader. The Bible teaches people to respect the authority of the government,[19] and children are expected to obey their parents.[20] Disobedience is often considered wrong, immoral, and sinful. People in authority decide the rules and the punishment for disobedience. The lack of respect for authority is a common moral emphasis for conservative Christians.

6. Purity and Sanctity vs. Degradation and Impurity

Yuk! A distorted face and a loud "yuk" indicate disgust. Disgust is close to a universal emotion. It is a deeply felt response commonly experienced in response to human and animal waste and bodily discharges. Many people have a hard time dealing with blood, urine, and feces. And many people keep their distance from those with bad breath or strong body odor. It's no surprise that ancient biblical laws expected people to bathe before entering the tabernacle.[21] Jesus extended the idea of cleanliness to include a clean mind, which we can think of as free from thoughts or plans to act immorally.[22]

---

19. 1 Pet 2:13.
20. Eph 6:1.
21. Exod 30:20.
22. Luke 11:39.

In the Bible we find that people with diseases were considered unclean. During the early days of Christianity, some people evidently labeled outsiders as unclean. To correct this harmful belief, Peter received a vision showing him that people should not be considered unclean.[23] The progression from observable yucky substances to labeling people, art, words, and behavior patterns as dirty or unclean happens imperceptibly and gradually permeates a culture such that people within a culture may not even realize how they mistreat people who do not follow their customs and traditions. Not surprisingly, various aspects of sexuality have also been labeled as dirty, impure, or even filthy and disgusting.

Learning from the experience of Peter, Christians can be careful to discern that which God considers unholy, impure, and degrading from that which is just a cultural difference that can have the effect of degrading other people or their behavior in ways having nothing to do with Christian morality.

SUMMARY AND CONCLUSION

In this chapter I provided two broad bases to illustrate the contribution of psychological science to morality. First, I reviewed six dimensions of human functioning using the acronym *SCOPES*. People are influenced in their moral actions by their *Spiritual* traditions and beliefs, *Cognition* (or thoughts) and long-term patterns of *Observable* behavior, also known as personality traits. They are also influenced by their *Physical* state, *Emotional* state, and the *Social* context, which includes people and even the time of day or day of the week.

In the second part of the chapter, I reviewed the six dimensions of morality researched by Jonathan Haidt and his colleagues. These six dimensions can help us understand how conservative and progressive Christians arrive at different conclusions about some social issues by emphasizing different dimensions. In general, progressive Christians emphasize the two dimensions of care and fairness and sometimes a third dimension of liberty. Conservative Christians tend to draw upon all six dimensions. Thus, in addition to the three that progressive Christians emphasize, conservative Christians refer to respect for authority, loyalty to one's church and faith tradition, and concerns about purity versus degradation.

23. Acts 10:9–16.

Now we can combine the two major sections of this chapter to understand how Christians make moral judgments. Christians form moral judgments by combining their understanding of biblical guidance with their understanding of human nature and one or more moral reasons consistent with those in their Christian culture. The six factors in the SCOPES model represent aspects of human nature. By considering the impact on each of the six factors, we can have a sense of how a moral judgment influences a person's wellbeing. Here's how you might frame a question: How does the moral judgment affect spiritual, cognitive, behavioral, physical, emotional, and social functioning?

ADDITIONAL RESOURCES

1. In 2014, the U.S. Senate Select Committee on Intelligence released a study of the detention and interrogation program conducted by the Central Intelligence Agency. Many people voiced their opinions about the morality of the program. Here is a link to the report: http://www.intelligence.senate.gov/study2014/sscistudy1.pdf.

2. In 2014, World Vision announced a decision to hire people in same-sex marriages. After two days of criticism, they reversed their decision. Here is a link to the story presented by *Christianity Today*: http://www.christianitytoday.com/ct/2014/march-web-only/world-vision-reverses-decision-gay-same-sex-marriage.html.

3. *The Hunger Games* film series includes several psychological factors linked to moral decisions. Here is a link to comments in *Wired Magazine*: http://www.wired.com/2014/11/mockingjay-violence-teens/.

4. In 2014, a grand jury reviewed evidence related to the death of Eric Garner, who died following an arrest that used force. The *National Review* article includes several dimensions of human functioning and reasons people use when speaking of the morality of the police action. Here is a link to the story: http://www.nationalreview.com/article/393933/staten-island-decision-andrew-c-mccarthy.

DISCUSSION QUESTIONS

1. See the report or a news story on the CIA interrogation program mentioned above. Try to analyze some of the arguments in favor

or against the interrogation procedures using the six dimensions of moral reasoning.

2. Imagine an 18-year-old woman who is pregnant as the result of rape. Consider how the six dimensions of the SCOPES model may help appreciate the sources of influence on her decision to keep the child or have an abortion. That is, how might her spirituality, thoughts, physiological state, feelings, past behavior, and social situation influence her final decision to keep the child or have an abortion?

3. Movies carry ratings to help people decide something about the content that may be objectionable. Think of a movie that might be of questionable value and evaluate the moral value using the six dimensions of morality proposed by Haidt and his colleagues.

4. Under what conditions does it seem morally reasonable to use high levels of force to prevent what looks like life-threatening violence? You might consider the case of Eric Garner referred to above or another contemporary case. Which of Haidt's six moral dimensions seem most important to you? For example, do you emphasize fairness, respect for authority, or other dimensions?

REFERENCES

Bancroft, John. "Sexual Desire and the Brain Revisited." *Sexual and Relationship Therapy* 25 (2010) 166–71.

Bateson, Melissa, et al. "Cues of Being Watched Enhance Cooperation in a Real-World Setting." *Biology Letters* 2 (2006) 412–14.

Bornstein, Brian H., and Monica K. Miller. "Does a Judge's Religion Influence Decision Making?" *Court Review* 45 (2008–2009) 112–15.

Danziger, Shai, et al. "Extraneous Factors in Judicial Decisions." *Proceedings of the National Academy of Sciences of the United States of America* (2011) 6889–92.

Haidt, Jonathan. *The Righteous Mind: Why Good People Are Divided By Politics and Religion*. New York: Pantheon, 2012.

Horsey, David. "John McCain has Moral Clarity about CIA Torture Report." December 11, 2014, http://www.latimes.com/opinion/topoftheticket/la-na-tt-john-mccain-cia-torture-20141211-story.html (accessed June 27, 2016).

Kahneman, Daniel. *Thinking, Fast and Slow*. New York: Farrar, Straus and Giroux, 2011.

Lipka, Michael. "Many U.S. Congregations Are Still Racially Segregated, but Things Are Changing." December 2014. http://www.pewresearch.org/fact-tank/ (accessed June 27, 2016).

Loftus, Elizabeth, and Katherine Ketcham. *Witness for the Defense*. New York: St. Martin's, 1991.

Pew Research Center. *The Global Religious Landscape*, 2012.

Senate Select Committee on Intelligence. *Committee Study of the Central Intelligence Agency's Detention and Interrogation Program*. United States Senate, 2014.

Sutton, Geoffrey W., and Martin W. Mittelstadt. "Loving God and Loving Others: Learning about Love from Psychological Science and Pentecostal Perspectives." *Journal of Christianity and Psychology* 31 (2012) 157–66.

Thompson-Cannino, Jennifer, et al. *Picking Cotton*. New York: St. Martin's, 2009.

Wilkinson, Michael, and Peter Althouse. *Catch the Fire: Soaking Prayer and Charismatic Renewal*. DeKalb: Northern Illinois University Press, 2014.

4

Sociological Foundations of Christian Morality

JOEL THIESSEN

CHAPTER OVERVIEW

IT IS MONDAY MORNING. Several questions swirl in my head following weekend activities with friends and family, worshiping in my local congregation, and following the news. Should safe injection sites exist? Is capital punishment morally appropriate? Are current approaches to immigration morally sound? Should gay marriage, abortion, euthanasia, or prostitution be legal? Should consumers pay an additional tax on fast food? Do countries have a moral obligation to get involved in the affairs of other nations through war, economic sanctions, or foreign aid? Should the wealthy be taxed more in order to aid the poor? As a sociologist and Christian I must think carefully about complex moral issues and in turn engage students in discussions about morality.

In this chapter I push you to think about the intersection between morality, Christianity, and sociology, whether you are a student, a professor, a church leader, or someone with a general interest in this subject. I will not tell you how to answer the moral dilemmas at hand. Rather I seek to equip you with sociological concepts that help you to navigate delicate moral topics from a Christian perspective. Below I survey four aspects of the evolving relationship between sociology, Christianity, and morality.[1] (1) I summarize the core elements of the sociological perspective. (2) I highlight the multiple streams within Christianity, sociology, and morality. (3) I examine ways that sociology can strengthen the Christian response to contemporary social issues. (4) I discuss power and oppression as gateways for thinking carefully and critically about the intersection between sociology, Christianity, and morality.

WHAT IS SOCIOLOGY?

Sociology is the scientific study of human society including social structures and institutions, like education or the family, and how individuals shape and are shaped by such structures. Drawing on methods such as surveys, interviews, or ethnographies, sociologists study real people in real situations. Since the discipline's inception (eighteenth century), sociologists have studied the shift from traditional to modern society. Their interests centered on morality, social norms, socialization, and social cohesion as industrialization, urbanization, the Enlightenment, and individualism swept across Europe and eventually the modern Western world. Upon studying these topics, sociologists made a key discovery about social life: we "see the general in the particular," meaning that general patterns in society are evident in the particulars of an individual's life.[2] Émile Durkheim, a French sociologist and key influencer in the discipline, is well known for his classic study on suicide.[3] He noted that, while individuals had particular reasons for committing suicide, such as loneliness, a lost job, or an illness, several social conditions were strongly correlated among those most likely to commit suicide. He observed that men, Protestants, the wealthy, and the unmarried were more likely to commit suicide when compared with women, Catholics or Jews, the poor, and those who were married. Why? It was because of one's social ties. The more socially connected one was, the more likely they were to turn for help rather than commit suicide. In other words, individual attitudes and behaviors cannot be reduced to individual agency alone, but must account for social structural patterns too.

Cultural and demographic attributes are another way to see how the general and particular relate. As a white male university professor in my

1. For a thorough exploration, see Hitlin and Vaisey, *Handbook*.
2. Berger, *Invitation to Sociology*.
3. Durkheim, *Suicide*.

thirties from Canada, I see and understand the world differently than a black female seamstress in her fifties who recently immigrated to the United States from Ghana. We come from social contexts with different assumptions tied to gender, age, race, and occupation and thus perceive and experience ourselves and others in a particular light. The 2014 tensions in Ferguson, Missouri, over race, crime, and the criminal justice system is just one example of this sociological fact. So too are Mary and Joseph's immediate reactions (to quietly separate) in Matt 1:18–25 following word of Mary's pregnancy. As you begin to think about the sociological perspective relative to morality, consider: How could sociology contribute to your approach to moral issues? How does your social position and social context shape your view of morality?

SOCIAL CONTEXT MATTERS

To accurately understand the interplay between Christianity, sociology, and morality, it is imperative to speak of these terms in their plural form. I teach at a faith-based university. I am frequently approached by students to offer "the Christian perspective" on a range of subjects such as economics or politics. I invariably flip the question to students, many of whom identify as Christian. Some suggest that Jesus would be a socialist because his priority is the marginalized and oppressed. Others say that Jesus would be a capitalist because he discouraged laziness and wants humans to live productive lives. Some do not think Jesus cares about a society's economic or political structure. If I invited my colleagues into the conversation, we too would hold differing views. Or consider denominational differences. Catholics, Methodists, and Baptists are distinguished by a particular view of God, the Bible, and the world. The point is that well-intentioned Christians land across a spectrum to define and respond to moral issues, and each thinks that they are honoring the truths and values within this "common" Christian faith.[4]

Sociologically, these variations can be explained by looking to one's demographic attributes such as age, gender, race, or economic status as well as social factors like denominational background, family upbringing, or country of origin (including social and historical context). For instance, empirical data reveal that people tend to construct religious ideas based on

---

4. See Niebuhr, *Christ and Culture*; Smith, *The Bible Made Impossible*; Hunter, *To Change the World*.

personal, social, and historical context.[5] An African American approaches slavery and oppression in the Bible or in society differently than does a Caucasian; so too does someone of low socioeconomic standing versus a position of economic privilege. The same applies throughout Scripture. Consider how one's background as a Jew or Gentile, male or female, rich or poor influenced their perception of Jesus. This observation does not negate common threads that unite the many expressions of Christianity. But there are multiple perspectives within Christianity; thus, to speak of *the* Christian worldview is misleading.

Sociology also contains multiple "camps," each with its own core assumptions about human beings, research methodology, and if or how research findings should be utilized by academics and the general public. For example, the structural functionalist paradigm, associated with Émile Durkheim, suggests that social institutions such as family, religion, or education fulfill unique functions that together enable society to thrive in a stable manner. Structural functionalists tend to reinforce conservative morals and values. Scholars like Kingsley Davis and Wilbert Moore argue that economic inequality serves a purpose in society: to motivate people to work harder.[6] Poverty is thus a result of poor choices by lazy individuals. Talcott Parsons argued in favor of traditional gender roles because of the perceived stability they bring in the home, the workplace, and society overall.[7] Methodologically, structural functionalists embrace value-neutrality, objectivity, and the scientific method. Knowledge is informed by facts that are positively observed with the senses via surveys or experiments rather than relying on opinion. Once research is complete, structural functionalists generally assume their task is complete; they do not aim to mobilize their research findings beyond the ivory tower.

In contrast, social conflict proponents, associated with German sociologist Karl Marx, maintain that society is fraught with inequality between the "haves" and the "have nots." Areas of inequality include gender, economics, race, or sexual orientation, to name a few. According to social conflict theorists, economic inequality exists because those in positions of economic and political power make decisions that benefit themselves at the expense of the poor (e.g., taxation laws). Concerning gender, females are marginalized at home and the workplace because of deeply entrenched

---

5. See Durkheim, *The Elementary Forms*.
6. Davis and Moore, "Some Principles," 242–49.
7. Parsons, "The American Family," 3–33.

patriarchal values in society. Methodologically, social conflict sociologists tend to rely on ethnography or interviews, and they are value-committed, meaning that sociology exists to better understand social inequalities and then to help eradicate social inequality based on sociological research. For social conflict theorists, equality is a moral issue; inequality is immoral.

This brings us to a focused sociological discussion on morality. Sociologists think differently about what is or is not moral, yet they share the sociological perspective that social context shapes how people define what is "normal" or "deviant." Christian Smith observes that "few people value individual freedom, for example, simply because they personally and idiosyncratically so happen to value it. People value freedom because they are embedded in a larger moral order that specifies what is good, right, true, just, and worthy in the context of which freedom is prized."[8] From family to education to religion to media to political discourse, humans are socialized to embrace different symbols, languages, values, and beliefs surrounding what a culture (e.g., nation) or subculture (e.g., religious group) believes is right or wrong, good or bad, beautiful or undesirable. This is why the politically left versus right differ so vehemently about the moral course of action relative to war, the justice system, immigration reform, same-sex marriage, or taxation. Each "side" is entrenched in social settings that reinforce a particular worldview that it believes is normal or right and demonize the opposing view as misguided propaganda. Social context also helps to explain why families of Asian descent might be appalled with North Americans who send their ageing parents to a nursing home rather than house and care for their parents themselves. These divergent approaches epitomize individualist versus collectivist orientations to social life that are infused with assumptions about morality.

Social norms are clearest when deviant attitudes or behaviors emerge. Breaching experiments—intentionally breaking social norms and witnessing people's reactions (e.g., talking to a stranger on an elevator)—are one way that sociologists measure how people define what is normal or deviant. When Rosa Parks, an African American woman, refused to give up her seat on the bus for a white person in 1955, she challenged prevailing social norms that privileged whites over blacks. The response—her arrest—reinforced dominant discourse over what was normal or deviant regarding race relations. At the same time, Rosa Parks acted out of what she and the African American community believed was a moral posture: racial equality

---

8. Smith, *Moral, Believing Animals*, 18.

between blacks and whites. Importantly, each position in this moral debate was reinforced in people's socialization contexts such as their families, education, media, and religion. Analogous illustrations of deviance clarifying social norms emerge when Jesus heals on the Sabbath in Mark 2:23–3:6 or speaks with a Samaritan woman in public in John 4:7–26.

An important question that sociologists ask is, "Who, in society, determines what moral claims are accepted?" And a related question is, "Why do they get to decide?" In the Rosa Park example white people held the power and privilege to decide what was accepted as moral or deviant so that black people were inferior on public transportation, in movie theaters, at restaurants, in the political process, and even before the law. As you contemplate moral issues of interest to you, consider who has the power to determine what is seen as moral or immoral. Why do they get to decide? Whose voice is not present in the debate?

Sociology reveals that moral beliefs and practices and social norms shift over time. Behaviors that were once deemed deviant are now normal and accepted, and punishments that were formally customary are now outlawed. Homosexual practices were once against the law in many western nations; this is no longer the case. Women were not allowed to vote in several regions of the world until relatively recently in history. Visible minorities were banned from many public spaces in the United States through the latter part of the twentieth century. Capital punishment was formerly practiced in Canada until protestors spoke out against this practice and the law changed in 1976. The same pattern extends to Christianity, where some attitudes and behaviors were previously upheld as immoral but now are acceptable. Some denominations banned women from wearing makeup or jewelry or holding positions of church leadership. Other groups kept individuals who were divorced from active membership and involvement in a congregation while others chastised drinking or smoking among church members. Today it is not difficult to find religious groups that have changed their positions in these and other ways.

As social context varies, morals can conflict with each other too. In Canada and the United States physical aggression is usually frowned upon. Parents discourage children from physically fighting to resolve their differences, teachers disapprove playground fights, and the law prohibits people from physically harming another. At the same time there are sanctioned contexts whereby violence is welcomed and encouraged. Take the National Hockey League or Ultimate Fighting as a couple of examples. Nations also endorse capital punishment and send their citizens to war as moral ways of resolving injustices. In 2011, I watched the news report of men, women, and children in America jubilantly celebrating the killing of Osama Bin Laden. The young children sitting beside me inquired about why people rejoiced over violence and murder. These celebrations conflicted with what they were taught regarding violence. The sociological lesson is that societies sometimes embrace competing moral values and when tensions between these values arise, nations, subgroups, and individuals prioritize some moral issues above others.

It is hopefully clear by now that Christianity, sociology, and moral norms are complex and fluid categories. One implication is that sociological principles should lead Christians to set aside proclamations of a single Christian response to moral decisions. For this reason it is wise to adopt a humble posture toward one's moral positions, to listen to and learn from other academic disciplines and theological perspectives. This does not mean that people avoid landing on a moral position, but the process to get there and the ways that one internalizes and externalizes their views will likely look different if humility is an anchoring point in the conversation.[9]

SOCIOLOGY STRENGTHENS A CHRISTIAN RESPONSE TO MORALITY

If Christians approach morality without a sociological framework, what might they miss in the process? The first is empirical data, particularly to "reveal differences between what people want to believe is happening in society and what actually is going on."[10] It is understandable that individuals get caught up with emotion, passion, and ideology when discussing morality, yet too often these factors can cloud the distinction between fiction and fact. For instance, many Christians denounce parenting by gays or lesbians on moral grounds, believing that a child benefits best from having a mother and a father. Sociological research affirms this claim, but when one looks closer at the empirical data, it is clear that having two parents that love each other is more beneficial to a child's long-term wellbeing than being raised by a single parent.[11] In other words, could divorce be a greater moral issue

---

9. Lyon, *Sociology and the Human Image*; Fraser and Campolo, *Sociology through the Eyes of Faith*; Smith, *The Bible Made Impossible*; Hunter, *To Change the World*.

10. Fraser and Campolo, *Sociology through the Eyes of Faith*, 61.

11. McDaniel and Tepperman, *Close Relations*, 190–91.

at stake rather than or alongside raising children by same-sex parents? I could provide countless examples where Christians think they are acting morally—by going on short-term mission trips, giving money to a homeless person, or supporting retribution forms of justice—when empirical data reveal that these approaches can exacerbate social problems. Without considering empirical evidence, Christians might (and do) hastily rush to attitudes and behaviors toward others for moral reasons, failing to see how their "Christian" actions might be morally problematic. Lest one think that empiricism is at odds with Christian faith and belief, Scripture is filled with examples to "come and see."[12] As Mark Noll denotes, "the message of the apostles did not primarily concern necessary truths of reason, but rather trust hard-won through experience . . . confidence in the promise unseen, in other words, rested on what had been seen . . . for any number of reasons, Christian realities do not make sense, until and unless they have been experienced."[13]

From empirical data arises a second benefit from sociology for Christians addressing moral issues: the ability to inform practical responses and public policy. Richard Perkins declares, "Any sociologist who tries to connect with social reality, but who remains uninvolved and uncommitted, has about as much chance of success as does an aspiring surgeon who refuses to cut open a patient."[14] Sociology arms us with empirical data to act in informed ways to help liberate individuals, communities, and societies from inequality, exploitation, and oppression of all kinds. For instance, based on empirical studies of those who are homeless, the conditions that contribute to homelessness, and the catalysts to get out of homelessness, policy makers can and do use sociological research to help curb homelessness. As another example, extensive sociological research on homegrown radicalization and terrorism is currently underway across North America. The data and analysis are and will be used by politicians, lawmakers, law enforcement, the criminal justice system, educators, religious leaders, and families to help prevent, identify, and respond to homegrown radicalization. Therefore, the Christian who values sociology will not approach morality merely out of personal passion or theological conviction, as important as these are, but will actively pursue tangible responses from an awareness of what the empirical data reveal.

12. See Matt 11:3–5, John 1:45–46, Acts 4:20, 1 John 1:1–3.
13. Noll, *Jesus Christ*, 50–52.
14. Perkins, "Values," 14.

Lastly, sociology aids individuals to be aware of the opportunities and constraints in their life and in other people's lives. This awareness is rooted in the ongoing sociological interest between structure and agency. A white boy who grows up in a wealthy family will have different educational, occupational, and relational opportunities and constraints than a black girl who comes from a poor background, due to how social structures privilege certain statuses and identities over another. In Canada, empirical evidence demonstrates that the general population, the media, and the legal system respond very differently toward a white female who is missing or murdered versus an Aboriginal female. In the former case there is greater urgency to help the white female "victim" while in the latter example there is a greater likelihood of blaming the Aboriginal woman for her troubles. As Christians come to grips with these social and systemic opportunities and constraints all based on empirical facts, the discourse surrounding morality should change. Would individual Christians, congregations, or denominations be as quick to blame the victim if a sociological perspective were employed? What would a compassionate and moral response look like? Would justice focus solely on the individual level, or would it address social, systemic, and structural variables as well? Asking questions such as these will strengthen the Christian's ability to holistically respond to the myriad of moral concerns in society.

In the end, much of sociology dovetails with areas of Christian commitment to individual and societal restoration and transformation. Speaking of Christian scholarship in general, Rodney Sawatzky claims that the goal is "not only to understand and to celebrate the creation as it is but also to participate in God's work of restoring and transforming the world."[15] Many areas of sociological inquiry revolve around inequalities and brokenness in society—crime, slavery, colonialism, political structures, poverty, racism, terrorism, the environment, healthcare, and education—to understand how and why such realities are the way they are and, in some contexts, to press toward concrete solutions for greater justice and peace in society. A Christian orientation to morality can benefit by paying attention to sociological questions, data, and analysis on numerous topics of mutual concern. Doing so can deepen and broaden the Christian community's thinking and ability to participate in God's redeeming and transforming activity in the world.

---

15. Sawatzky, "Prologue: The Virtue," 10.

AN APPLICATION: POWER AND OPPRESSION

Applying sociology to Christians making moral decisions could easily go in several worthwhile directions that might include economics, gender, sexuality, education, race and ethnicity, or politics. I briefly focus here on two related subjects that are central in sociological study and that have notable theological bearing: power and oppression.

What does it mean for a Christian in a position of power to think and act morally? Scripture is full of references that "the last shall be first and the first shall be last"[16] and leaders should "take the posture of a servant."[17] Jesus speaks clearly about rulers showing mercy too.[18] In his book, *To Change the World*, James Davison Hunter showcases Jesus' approach to power, which is rooted in an intimate and submissive relationship with God the Father. Jesus rejected the status, reputation, and privilege that came with power. Compassion was also central to Jesus' leadership, and he opened his arms widely to all, regardless of background.[19]

What do these Christian moral norms for power look like in tangible terms? Knowing that certain groups in society are systemically disadvantaged and thus have fewer choices and personal agency relative to the social structures at large, what is the Christian's moral responsibility with their position of power? Framed another way, mindful that those in positions of power have more agency and choice to do as they please, how best should one use that agency?

- For the boss in a work environment, which is morally superior: to fire someone who repeatedly shows up to work late or offer a second or third or fourth chance at redemption?

- For a politician, which is the higher moral response: to pass laws that provide financial assistance to single parents or abandon financial assistance so as to discourage people from having children outside of marriage or divorcing?

- For the judge, is it morally preferable to sentence a young adult to retributive forms of justice or restorative forms of justice? Further,

---

16. For example, Matt 9:33–35; 20:16.
17. For example, Luke 14:11 and Phil 2:5–8.
18. For example, Matt 18:21–35 and Luke 18:1–14.
19. Hunter, *To Change the World*, 188–93.

how would information about the person's family background (e.g., lone parent versus two-parent family), race, socioeconomic status, or education level inform the judge's handling of the situation?

Power extends beyond formalized contexts too. I have privileges in society simply because I am male, white, and wealthy by global standards. How best should I use this power? What responsibilities could or should I have relative to women or visible minorities in society (e.g., at home, at work, in my neighborhood, or in my church)? Economically, what is my moral responsibility to those who are not as well off? In what ways are you in a position of power, and what is your moral responsibility with that power? If you are not in a position of power, what might your relationship to those in power look like? Is it moral to submit to those over you? Should you protest against those in power? How might social context nuance your responses, whether you are in the home with parents, in the workplace with a boss, in a church with a pastor, or in society with a political leader? According to Hunter, "What this means is that faithful Christian witness is fated to exist in the tension between the historical and the transcendent; between the social realities that press on human existence and the spiritual and ethical requirements of the gospel; between the morality of the society in which Christian believers live and the will of God."[20]

Oppression is a theme related to power. Morals and norms can reinforce social solidarity and belonging in a group, but they can also function to exclude people from a group. Ironically, while Christianity calls on oppressors to cease their repressive ways and to seek peace, justice, unity, and welfare for all—interests that align with many prominent concerns within sociological inquiry—one must ask, "In what ways have Christians used morality as a way to exclude and oppress?"[21] In Canada, several Christian groups were responsible for forcibly removing Aboriginal children from their families and placing them in residential schools in an attempt to "Christianize and civilize" them. This is one of the saddest chapters in Canadian history. Christianity, among other religious groups, is widely recognized as one of the most patriarchal social organizations in the world; (e.g., women are banned from religious leadership in many denominations and congregations). In the minds of many, Christianity is synonymous with a homophobic culture, evident as Christians disassociate themselves from

---

20. Ibid., 183.
21. Lyon, *Sociology and the Human Image*, 205.

gay family members and congregations excommunicate gays and lesbians from their midst.[22] When it comes to race, research clearly shows that Sunday mornings are the most racially segregated hour of the week.[23]

It is true that Christians and other religious individuals and groups adopt an array of beliefs and practices that are generally seen as socially beneficial.[24] Still, relatively irreligious individuals and groups are growing in number across the modern Western world, and studies increasingly show strong levels of morality in these contexts; religious individuals do not have the corner on the morality market.[25] Moreover, as just demonstrated, Christians are sometimes the oppressors in society. Therefore, if Christians are called to pursue justice and mercy in society,[26] and to prophetically call out oppressors in the process, part of the discussion entails that the Christian community takes a careful look in the mirror.

These observations compel me to raise several pertinent theological questions. Is it fair to compare modern day Christian engagement in some moral domains with the Pharisees who Jesus actively spoke against? What are the essentials of the Christian faith? Are the topics noted above core or peripheral to Christian belief and practice? What is one to make of the social norms and morals encouraged in the Ten Commandments,[27] the Sermon on the Mount,[28] or throughout Pauline theology relative to today's social context? How do modern day moral concerns intersect with foundational documents in Christianity, such as the Apostles' Creed or the Nicene Creed?[29] What would it look like to pursue greater equality along gender, sexual orientation, race, or economic lines? How does one balance grace and truth,[30] especially when supposed moral values stand in conflict with each other? Would equality contravene theological truths or values? On what basis do you approach these questions? How does your social context

---

22. Kinnaman and Lyons, *unChristian*, 91–119.

23. Emerson and Woo, *People of the Dream*, 5.

24. See, for example, Bowen, *Christians in a Secular World*; Cnaan, *The Invisible Caring Hand*; Putnam and Campbell, *American Grace*; Smidt, *Religion as Social Capital*; Wuthnow, *Saving America?*

25. See, for example, Zuckerman, *Faith No More*; Zuckerman, *Society without God*.

26. Mic 6:8.

27. Exod 20:2–17.

28. Matt 5–7.

29. See Noll, *Jesus Christ*.

30. John 1:14–17.

shape your response, and what might you learn from those coming from a different social position? These questions and the subsequent answers are not straightforward, and they demand careful and critical sociological and theological engagement. Committing to this rigorous activity, however, will strengthen one's ability to approach morality with the level of nuance and complexity that the subject so richly deserves. In turn, this exercise will help you to deal with specific moral dilemmas surrounding gender, sexuality, war, economics, race, the environment, addictions, and so forth.

CHAPTER SUMMARY

In summary, sociology is principally interested in scientifically studying human behavior, including the ways that individuals and society impact each other. A sociological perspective privileges empiricism as a way of knowing and has the potential to shape how individuals and social institutions evolve over time, for better or worse. When considering the ways that Christianity, sociology, and morality interact, it is essential to think of these ideas in their many forms. To speak of these concepts in the singular misses the profound theoretical and empirical insights that sociology has to offer about the power of social context on people's attitudes, experiences, and behaviors. In turn, it is valuable to hold one's sociological, theological, and moral positions, whatever they may be, with a degree of humility and openness toward other perspectives. As a sociologist and a Christian, I remain hopeful because of the overlap between sociological interests and the biblical drama of the creation, fall, redemption, and future age: "We may also see our own task as one of recalling sociology to creation priorities, through the renewing work of Christ, aware of the distorting effects of the fall but spurred on by the hope of the coming kingdom of God."[31]

ADDITIONAL RESOURCES

1. Tony Campolo is one of the most recognized Christian sociologists who has written and spoken extensively on several moral issues in contemporary society. This link includes access to his publications, multimedia presentations, and activist initiatives, among other resources: http://tonycampolo.org/.

31. Lyon, *Sociology and the Human Image*, 193.

CHRISTIAN MORALITY—PART ONE

2. This infograph captures competing ideas over the "higher" morality concerning safe injection sites: http://www.macleans.ca/wp-content/uploads/2013/07/safe-injection-sites.jpg. Here is an interview with a leading Christian proponent of safe injection sites: http://www.theglobeandmail.com/news/british-columbia/qa-nurse-offers-christian-defence-of-insite-facility/article579845/.

3. The United States is the only industrialized country to not provide paid leave for parents of newborns. Here is a comparison of how the United States compares with other countries: http://www.huffingtonpost.com/2013/05/10/paid-leave-maternity-_n_3253895.html.

4. Ron Sider, founder of *Evangelicals for Social Action*, circulated a theological reflection on homosexuality in 2014, a response that reflects many of the complexities highlighted in this chapter: http://www.christianitytoday.com/ct/2014/november-web-only/ron-sider-tragedy-tradition-and-opportunity-in-homosexualit.html?paging=off.

DISCUSSION QUESTIONS

1. How does your social context inform how you view various moral issues? How and why might your perspective vary from someone who does not share your demographic traits?

2. In what ways do empirical data inform your responses to morality? How might you give more space to empiricism, and where would you look to find empirical data on an area of moral interest to you?

3. What are the limits of sociology for dealing with morality from a Christian perspective?

4. Can you think of examples where moral norms in Scripture potentially conflict with each other? What about competing Christian understandings of certain moral issues in contemporary society? How could or should Christians resolve these tensions?

REFERENCES

Berger, Peter. *Invitation to Sociology: A Humanistic Perspective*. Garden City, NY: Anchor, 1963.

Bowen, Kurt. *Christians in a Secular World: The Canadian Experience*. Montréal: McGill-Queen's University Press, 2004.

Cnaan, Ram A. *The Invisible Caring Hand: American Congregations and the Provision of Welfare*. New York: New York University Press, 2002.

Davis, Kingsley, and Wilbert Moore. "Some Principles of Stratification." *American Sociological Review* 10 (1945) 242–49.

Durkheim, Emile. *Suicide: A Study in Sociology*. New York: Free, 1951.

———. *The Elementary Forms of the Religious Life: A Study in Religious Sociology*. New York: Free, 1915.

Emerson, Michael O., and Rodney M. Woo. *People of the Dream: Multiracial Congregations in the United States*. Princeton: Princeton University Press, 2006.

Fraser, David A., and Tony Campolo. *Sociology through the Eyes of Faith*. New York: HarperCollins, 1992.

Hitlin, Steven, and Stephen Vaisey, eds. *Handbook of the Sociology of Morality*. New York: Springer, 2013.

Hunter, James Davison. *To Change the World: The Irony, Tragedy, and Possibility of Christianity in the Late Modern World*. New York: Oxford University Press, 2010.

Kinnaman, David, and Gabe Lyons. *unChristian: What a New Generation Really Thinks about Christianity . . . and Why it Matters*. Grand Rapids: Baker, 2007.

Lyon, David. *Sociology and the Human Image*. Downers Grove, IL: InterVarsity, 1983.

McDaniel, Susan A., and Lorne Tepperman. *Close Relations: An Introduction to the Sociology of Families*. 5th ed. Toronto: Pearson, 2015.

Niebuhr, H. Richard. *Christ and Culture*. New York: Harper & Row, 1951.

Noll, Mark. *Jesus Christ and the Life of the Mind*. Grand Rapids: Eerdmans, 2011.

Parsons, Talcott. "The American Family: Its Relations to Personality and to the Social Structure." In *Family, Socialization, and Interaction Process*, edited by Talcott Parsons and Robert F. Bales, 3–33. Glencoe, IL: Free, 1955.

Perkins, Richard. "Values, Alienation, and Christian Sociology." *Christian Scholars Review* 15 (1985) 8–27.

Putnam, Robert, and David Campbell. *American Grace: How Religion Divides and Unites Us*. New York: Simon & Schuster, 2010.

Sawatzky, Rodney J. "Prologue: The Virtue of Scholarly Hope." In *Scholarship and Christian Faith: Enlarging the Conversation*, edited by Douglas Jacobsen and Rhonda Hustedt Jacobsen, 3–14. New York: Oxford University Press, 2004.

Smidt, Corwin, ed. *Religion as Social Capital: Producing the Common Good*. Waco, TX: Baylor University Press, 2003.

Smith, Christian. *The Bible Made Impossible: Why Biblicism is Not a Truly Evangelical Reading of Scripture*. Grand Rapids: Brazos, 2012.

———. *Moral, Believing Animals: Human Personhood and Culture*. New York: Oxford University Press, 2003.

Wuthnow, Robert. *Saving America? Faith-Based Services and the Future of Civil Society*. Princeton: Princeton University Press, 2004.

Zuckerman, Phil. *Faith No More: Why People Reject Religion*. New York: Oxford University Press, 2012.

———. *Society without God: What the Least Religious Nations Can Tell Us about Contentment*. New York: New York University Press, 2008.

5

Jesus, Empire, and Christian Ethics

Implications for the Moral Critique of Mass Incarceration in the United States

PETER ALTHOUSE

THEOLOGICAL ETHICS, OR MORAL theology, is a sub-discipline in theology that seeks to provide a framework for how one should live. Jesus' aphorism that sums up the Law, "Love God with all your heart, mind, body and soul and love your neighbor as yourself,"[1] is the basis for theological engagement of morality. However, in the Enlightenment and modernity, ethics have been relegated to the individual and privatized along with faith. Under Descartes's "thinking self" and Kant's categorical imperative regarding what an individual ought to do, moral decision-making has become a private affair. Public faith and public morality is eschewed, or at least frowned upon, and thought of as something that should be separated from the social sphere. Yet theology has developed resources for engaging the public sphere with ethical demands in order to address the second half of Jesus' aphorism, "Love your neighbor as yourself." Social ethics and political theology as disciplines hold that the good news of the gospel insists all persons regardless of race, ethnicity, gender, and class have dignity rooted in the *imago dei*, and from this dignity stem fundamental human rights. Moral theology provides resources and directives that are rooted in Scripture and

---

1. Paraphrase of Mark 12:30–31.

in theological tradition to address social justice concerns when this dignity and these rights are violated. Often, the violation of human dignity and rights occurs in a social, political, and/or economic context and must be resisted through public endeavors.

Empire and postcolonial readings of Scripture are developing methodologies that have consequences for theological ethics. Rooted in a multidisciplinary approach, empire/postcolonial studies place Jesus in the context of Roman occupation of Palestine and tease out Jesus' prophetic voice and that of his followers against the empire in order to resist the claims of Caesar's divinity and the perpetuation of dehumanization, enslavement, and violence by the Roman forces. The implication for theological ethics is that claiming personal moral integrity in spiritual piety as the sole requirement of Christian morality, while at the same time overlooking the injustices taking place in the world, is morally deficient. I will make the case that Christians must be active in engaging world injustices in light of the liberating impulse of the gospel. Jesus fought against the worldly powers of his day in subversive ways and paid the ultimate price of execution by crucifixion. At the same time, Jesus proclaimed the renewal of the covenant. To be followers of Christ means that we too are called to offer a prophetic voice in the face of injustices around the world rather than remain mute in a way that serves to reinforce those injustices. Political theology is a theological discipline that provides resources responding to social injustices in whatever form in a way that values the coming of Christ's kingdom reign.

In order to argue my case, I have drawn together two strands. The first is an analysis of Jesus and the Gospels in the context of the Roman Empire, specifically drawing on the work of University of Massachusetts distinguished professor Richard A. Horsley. My reason for looking at the Gospels is that good Christian theology and practice, in the truest sense of the word, is rooted in the primacy and normativity of Scripture. Recent developments in empire/postcolonial studies have shed new light on the meaning of the Gospels and their implications for today. Jesus' teachings and actions, and that of the writers who produced the New Testament documents, were directed in part against Roman rule and the cult of Caesar. Once this context is brought to light, then Jesus can be seen as a prophet acting in the manner of the prophets of old in critiquing the ruling powers that place the people in disadvantage, and the Gospels can be seen as a form of political resistance as a moral obligation for a people in covenant relationship.[2] In other words, the Gospels and much of the New Testament are resistance literature.

The second strand is an attempt to apply the resistance interpretation to a current moral injustice in America today—mass incarceration. *Mass incarceration* is a term that describes the injustice of the American criminal system that disproportionately targets African Americans and Latinos/as for incarceration for non-violent crimes for which they are more likely to be imprisoned and remain in prison for longer periods of time. Mass incarceration is more than simply imprisonment but consists of multiple systems that include policing, judicial policies and processes, incarceration and post-incarceration practices, and disenfranchisement that systematically maintains what Michelle Alexander calls "new Jim Crow" racism.[3] Mass incarceration has the effect of enslaving a race of Americans without using the language of slavery or racism. In order to show the socio-moral failure of the American judicial system and the ethical call to social change, I will draw connections between the Roman Empire of Jesus' day, which dominated, terrorized, and subjugated the people of Palestine, and the practices of the American judicial system, which dominates and subjugates people of color in our day.

THE GOSPEL IN THE CONTEXT OF THE EMPIRE

Scholars of religion have begun to appreciate the role that the Roman Empire played in the life of Jesus and the social-political context of ancient Palestine. Richard Horsley, who will be my main interlocutor in this regard, has made important contributions to the understanding of nascent Christianity in the Mediterranean. The Roman Empire is not simply a political backdrop to the message of Jesus and the Gospels, but the focus of a sustained resistance and condemnation by the gospel writers. Ancient Palestine was the locus of brutal Roman conquests and reconquests, which sparked a series of messianic movements as a means of covenant renewal, resistance, and revolutionary attempts. Moreover, in order to maintain the hegemony of the empire, the cult of Caesar that placed the emperor alongside other deities to be worshipped as divine was a particularly disturbing pill to swallow for the different Jewish peoples who believed YHWH was

---

2. See, for instance, Bruegemann, *The Prophetic Imagination*.

3. Alexander, *The New Jim Crow*; Wacquant, "When Ghetto," 82–120.

the one and only true God. The context of Jesus' life and death as recorded in the Gospels especially is one of resistance to the dehumanizing and marginalizing practices of the empire.

Conquests and Resistance

The historical context in which the Gospels were written was the Jerusalem revolt in 66 CE, when the people of Jerusalem revolted against the temple priests who were Roman collaborators, expelled of Roman troops from the city, and killed the remaining Roman garrison. The Roman reaction was one of total desolation when Vespasian and Titus slaughtered and enslaved the people in the surrounding villages of Galilee and Judea and finally reconquered Jerusalem and destroyed the temple in 70 CE. The destruction of the temple is a focal point of all three synoptic Gospels, and Jesus is inserted as the temple's replacement.[4] However, numerous conquests and revolts occurred both prior to and after the destruction of the temple. In fact, the history of the Israelite people was one of domination by one empire or another, including the Assyrian, Babylonian, and Greek. Under the Greek Empire, a faction of the priestly class in collaboration with Antiochus Epiphanes transformed Jerusalem's temple-state into a Greek-style city-state that eventually led to the Maccabean revolt, when the Hasmonean priestly family allied with the Judean people and scribes to overthrow Seleucid domination. However, the Hasmoneans consolidated their own power through a series of compromises and treaties with the empire.

The domination of the Roman Empire over Palestine began with Pompey, who took over Syria and Mesopotamia in 64–63 BCE. He later marched into Palestine and, when met with resistance from a faction of the Hasmoneans, besieged Jerusalem and the temple. Soon after, the Roman Empire was racked by civil war until Julius Caesar's adopted son Octavian emerged victorious against Anthony in the battle of Actium. At this point, he adopted the name Augustus (meaning revered or highly honored) and was acclaimed by the empire as "savior" who brought in the reign of "peace and prosperity."[5] Empire control over Palestine was maintained through brutal conquests and reconquests over the area and the establishment of client-kings (most notable was Herod and his son) who selected and colluded with the high priest and temple priests in order to maintain socioeconomic

---

4. See Wright, *The Challenge of Jesus*, 65, 110.
5. Horsley, *Jesus and Empire*, 20.

control. In 52 BCE, Crassus slaughtered, enslaved, and devastated the area of Magdala, and a few years later took slaves from four towns in Judea, including Emmaus. Crassus appointed King Herod in 40–37 to subjugate and maintain control over the area.[6] In 4 BCE, Rome reconquered the area near Nazareth, around the time of Jesus' birth, which may have been the reason why Mary and Joseph fled to Egypt. Moreover, both Herod and his son Antipas took exorbitant amounts of revenue (tribute) in order to build Roman-like cities such as Caesarea (named after Caesar), Sepphoris, and Tiberius. The peasants were economically devastated, not only being required to pay tithe to the temple, but also required to pay tribute to Herod and Rome.[7] Even after the temple was destroyed, Simon bar Kakhba, who was acclaimed messiah, led a revolt against Roman domination in 132–35 CE. Messianic movements were prophetic protests and resistance against the inhumane and devastating conditions of Palestine.

The dynamics of the empire were such that while the center of power in Rome was relatively stable and without a need for military presence, the frontiers were maintained with Roman legions through the use of violence that was meant to thwart any form of resistance.[8] Through a system of patronage, wealth in the form of tribute moved from the outskirts of the empire into the coffers of the Roman elite. Rome would celebrate its military conquests through extravagant celebrations in order to extract *fides* or *pistes*—"loyalty"—from its subjugated peoples.[9] Crucifixions, mass slaughter, and enslavement were particularly brutal methods for terrorizing the subjugated. Roman generals and governors assigned to Judea and Galilee used crucifixions to terrorize the inhabitants and deter any form of resistance. In retaliation for the revolt in 4 BCE, Roman general Varus crucified two thousand men. Felix (52–60) and Festus (60–62) crucified countless bandits as an example. Anyone who protested, rebelled against Roman rule, or was an actual bandit was labeled as a bandit, including the misnamed "thief" who was crucified with Jesus. Just prior to the destruction of the temple in 70 CE, Titus had so many prisoners crucified that they ran out of crosses and space to erect the crosses.[10]

---

6. Ibid., 60–61.
7. Mark 12:13–17.
8. Ibid., 22.
9. Ibid., 26; also, Horsley, "Introduction," 88–95; ibid., 140.
10. Horsley, *Jesus and Empire*, 27–29.

JESUS, EMPIRE, AND CHRISTIAN ETHICS

The Cult of Caesar.

In order to maintain ideological and hegemonic control over the empire, the cult of Caesar was established—the cult that proclaimed Caesar as god and established blood sacrifices as rituals of devotion. This inscription dated to 9 BCE was from the Provincial Assembly of Asia Minor and gave expression to the cult of the emperor, which directs honor and worship to Caesar depicted as the "savior" who brought "peace and prosperity" under the *Pax Romana*:

> The most divine Caesar . . . we should consider equal to the Beginning of all things . . . for when everything was falling [into disorder] and tending toward dissolution, he restored it once more and gave to the whole world a new era; Caesar . . . the common good Fortune of all. . . . The beginning of life and vitality . . . All the cities unanimously adopt the birthday of Caesar as the new beginning of the year. . . . Whereas Providence, which has regulated our whole existence . . . has brought our life to the climax of perfection in giving us [the emperor] Augustus, whom it [Providence] filled with strength for the welfare of men, and who being sent to us and our descendent as Savior, has put an end to war and has set all things in order; and [whereas,] having become [god] manifest (*phaneis*), Caesar has fulfilled all the hopes of earlier times . . . in surprising all the benefactors who preceded him . . . and whereas, finally, the birthday of the god [Augustus] has been for the whole world the beginning of good news (*euangelion*) concerning him [therefore] let a new era begin from his birth.[11]

The good news of the gospel was attributed to Caesar, who was described as the "son of God," "divine," "the beginning of all things," the "beginning and vitality of life," and "savior." Caesar's *Pax Romana* was propagated as an era of peace and prosperity. However, the emperor's peace was bought with violence and degradation.

Empire Resistance in the Demoniac of Gerasene

The subversive resistance to Roman imperial rule and the cult of the emperor is found in Scripture in rhetorical codes. Overt and active resistance is the tip of the iceberg, but what lies below are hidden forms of resistance. Drawing on James C. Scott, Horsley makes a distinction between "official

---

11. As quoted in Horsley, *Jesus and Empire*, 23–24.

CHRISTIAN MORALITY—PART ONE

transcript" and "hidden transcript." In the context of conflict, the speech and behavior of subjugated peoples are coerced by the dominating elites, and communication supports the structures of power in written documents, or official transcript. However, the hidden transcripts produced by the subjugated, critique the powers of the elite. Their purpose is to keep anger and resentment alive and occasionally fuel movements of protest and resistance. The hidden transcript of the Israelite people is rooted in the deliverance motif of the covenant.[12]

The demoniac of Gerasene is a case in point.[13] There is a tendency among conservative Christians especially to literalize and/or spiritualize this passage in order to interpret it in mythological terms as the forces of darkness against the forces of light. However, when placed within the historical context of the Roman imperial order, its meaning begins to emerge.

The narrative begins with a statement that they travelled to the other side of the Sea of Galilee. "The other side" is not simply a reference to the opposite side of the sea, but that Jesus and his disciples travelled into an area controlled by the Gentiles (that is, the Romans and their collaborators) where swine are raised in violation of the Mosaic code. Jesus' audience would have immediately understood the implications of the statement in which Jesus and his disciples are ritually unclean. Jesus is immediately accosted by a man with an unclean spirit, reinforcing the violation of Mosaic Law. The man could not be bound or kept in chains, an image depicting his disarray from subjugation and his resistance to enslavement. The Galileans who heard this story would be reminded immediately of social trauma they had experienced when the Galileans were slaughtered, enslaved, and devastated in Magdala in 52 BCE, in 40–37 BCE by Rome-appointed king Herod, and by the Roman reconquest of the area near Nazareth in 4 BCE.[14] If the audience did not yet get that this story was a story of resistance to Roman rule, then the statement "my name is Legion for we are many" would be close to a direct statement of resistance in a conquered land. Legion is a reference to Roman troops. The rest of the passage is peppered with military images. "Legion" is "dismissed" and then enter a "troop" (herd) of swine. They "charge" (rush) as if into battle, but are then "drowned in

---

12. Horsley, *Jesus and Empire*, 53–54.
13. Mark 5:1–20.
14. Horsley, *Jesus and Empire*, 60.

the sea." The sea alludes to the Israelite exodus from Egypt when Pharaoh's armies were drowned in the Red (Reed) Sea (see Exod 15:1–4).[15]

The linking of the unclean spirit or demons to the Roman military is further supported by evidence from the Dead Sea Scrolls. The Qumran Essenes protested against imperial rule and wickedness of the Roman-collaborating high priests. Their new exodus to the Dead Sea and covenant rule in Judea was a passive resistance to empire. They conceived the Romans ("Kittim") as the embodiment of satanic forces. They practiced symbolic ritual warfare in anticipation of the cosmic battle between the demonic forces and Kittim on the one side and the Essenes and the forces of light on the other.[16] It should not be lost to the reader that the Qumran community was utterly destroyed during the Roman campaign that destroyed the Jerusalem Temple.

I need not belabor the point. The Gospels are peppered with narratives of resistance to empire rule if one has the eyes to see. The Gospels were written around the time of Rome's invasion and destruction of the temple, and the early Christians were caught up in the problems of empire. Other examples of empire resistance include narratives of tribute, temple destruction, demoniacs and healings, to name just a few. Followers of Jesus and the New Testament writers used rhetorical codes to make this claim, using terminology ascribed to Caesar for Jesus. Faith, Gospel, son of God, bringer of peace, beginning of all things, etc., words ascribed to Caesar and his empire, were made of Jesus and the church. Jesus himself was part of a resistance movement against empire. To borrow a phrase from Scott McKnight and Joseph B. Modica, resistance against the empire was an early confession, proclaiming, "Jesus is Lord, Caesar is not."[17] One need only look at the manner of his death to realize this fact. Crucifixion was used as a brutal form of torture and death for any form of resistance and as an example to would be revolutionaries.

MORAL CRITIQUE OF MASS INCARCERATION

At this point I would like to shift the discussion in order to focus on the implications of empire resistance in the life of Jesus and the message of the Gospels for the world today. Numerous opportunities offer themselves

15. Ibid., 100–101.
16. Ibid.; also Horsley, *Religion and the Empire*, 81.
17. McKnight and Modica, *Jesus Is Lord Caesar Is Not*.

both historically and today. European colonial powers such as France, Great Britain, Germany, and Spain, etc., assumed colonial control over much of the world, including the Americas. The United States adopted the role of empire after WWII and became a world superpower in its cold war with the Soviet Union. The U.S. continues to exert its position as empire through policies of intervention in the Middle East. However, at home the policies and practices of mass incarceration for a segment of its citizens, particularly African Americans and Latinos/as, needs to come under the moral critique as a form of empire domination. Mass incarceration is not simply the imprisonment of criminals, but the linking of systems that label and place at a substantial disadvantage people of color for mostly nonviolent drug crimes, which were treated as a medical issue forty years ago. Mass incarceration of African Americans is also disproportionate because white citizens who use drugs at the same rate are much less likely to be processed through the criminal justice system.

The National Council of Churches in Christ USA has taken up the crisis of mass incarceration as an issue of social justice in need of a moral theological response. These are a few of the facts regarding the current state of mass incarceration. The numbers are startling:

- The U.S. consists of 5 percent of the world's population but 25 percent of the world's imprisoned population. The U.S. incarcerates more people than all western nations and most totalitarian regimes.
- The U.S. confines 2.3 million people in federal and state prisons and jails (or 1 in 99 adults).
- 65 million people are under correctional control on probation, parole, or suffering the impact of a criminal record.
- 93 percent of people in prison are male; 7 percent are female.
- 1 in 9 young African Americans between the ages of 20 and 34 are incarcerated.
- 1 in 3 black men has a lifetime likelihood of being incarcerated, compared to 1 in 6 Latino and 1 in 17 white men.
- As of 2012, 38 percent of people in state and federal prisons were black, 35 percent were white, 21 percent Hispanic.
- 32 percent of black males have a chance of being incarcerated at some point in their lives, 17 percent Hispanics, 6 percent whites.

- In 2012 the rate of imprisonment for black women was 2.5 times higher than for white women; the rate for Hispanic women was 14 times higher.
- More than 60 percent of the people in prison are people of color. Black men are 6 times more likely to be incarcerated than white men, and Hispanic men are 2.4 times more likely.
- For women, the lifetime likelihood of incarceration is 1 in 18 for black, 1 in 45 for Latina and 1 in 111 for white.
- The cause for the steep rise in incarceration since 1980 is the so-called "War on Drugs."
- Over half of all federal prisoners are incarcerated for nonviolent drug offenses.
- Nearly half (47 percent) of people incarcerated in state prisons was for non-violent drug, property, or public order crimes.
- Punishment continues after incarceration, as evidenced by prohibiting ex-felons or their families from public housing benefits and barring them from federal assistance, including food stamps. They also experience employment discrimination and general disenfranchisement—all of which contribute to high rates of recidivism.
- People convicted of drug offenses were 17 percent of state prison inmates in 2010 and 48 percent of federal prison inmates in 2011.[18]

Marc Mauer used the term *mass incarceration* to describe a penal system that links together multiple systems that not only put people behind bars, but label people as felons. Once labeled as ex-felons, they experience a system of impoverishment produced by a denial of social services, deprivation of resources, and loss of social rights. In many states, felons are denied workplace licenses and driver's licenses, low income housing, welfare subsidies such as food stamps and voting rights, sometimes for life. These punitive practices contribute to a higher rate of recidivism. Moreover, families of the incarcerated suffer greater levels of impoverishment because they lack financial means and social support necessary for family

---

18. Crokett, "Starter Kit," http://nationalcouncilofchurches.us/images/CEEF-FLD_2015_SKTL_MI.pdf; data from "Facts about Prison and People in Prison," last modified January 2014, http://sentencingproject.org/doc/publications/inc_Facts%20About%20Prisons.pdf; "The Sentencing Project," http://www.sentencingproject.org/template/page.cfm?id=122; Levad, *Redeeming a Prison Society*, 11.

development.[19] David Garland identifies two distinct features for a criminal system to be considered a system of mass incarceration: first, the rate of incarceration and size of prison populations must exceed historical rates and be higher than other comparable nations; and second, incarceration ceases to be about individual criminal offenses and becomes a system of imprisoning whole groups of people. The criminal justice system in the U.S. qualifies on both accounts as a system of mass incarceration.[20] The high levels of incarceration, when compared historically and globally, and the high percentage of people of color imprisoned in relation to population indicate that mass incarceration is a serious moral problem in the U.S.

Mass incarceration is also identified as a "prison industrial complex" because it links together multilayered systems of policing, criminal proceedings, incarceration, and post-incarceration processes such as parole and pardon and because major corporations are profiting from mass incarceration. The prison industrial complex is financially disadvantageous to the states that must funnel more and more taxpayer dollars into prisons and other criminal justice systems due to the increased number of prisoners and the longer mandated prison terms. This takes money away from other institutions that could help alleviate incarceration, such as rehabilitation, education, and social support systems. More disturbing is that governments in their effort to finance mass incarceration have privatized federal and state prisons, many of which guarantee 90 percent occupancy rate.[21] Supermax prisons have been built and have developed cost-saving tactics through overcrowding, incapacitation (in which a prisoner must remain in his cell for twenty-three hours a day), and substandard—and even denial of—mental and medical care to the point that the California Supreme Court has deemed them a violation of human dignity.[22] Also, to recoup imprisonment costs, states are charging prisoners fees for being incarcerated, but more concerning is that prisoners are seen as cheap labor for the industrial expansion of production. As industrial and manu-

---

19. Mauer, *Race to Incarcerate*.

20. Garland, "Introduction," 1–3.

21. See, for instance, https://www.aclu.org/blog/cca-trying-take-over-world; http://usatoday30.usatoday.com/news/nation/story/2012-03-01/buying-prisons-require-high-occupancy/53402894/1; https://www.washingtonpost.com/blogs/govbeat/wp/2013/09/19/are-governments-incentivizing-longer-prison-terms/; and https://www.washingtonpost.com/posteverything/wp/2015/04/28/how-for-profit-prisons-have-become-the-biggest-lobby-no-one-is-talking-about/.

22. Simon, *Mass Incarceration on Trial*, 133.

facturing jobs have been transported overseas in the search for cheap labor, prisoners have become a source of cheap labor. Prisoners are used to produce consumer goods and services for as low as thirty cents an hour and are denied basic civil rights and workplace regulations such as minimum wage, safe workplace environments, and unionization.[23] What should not be lost in this practice is that the majority of prisoners are people of color in prison for nonviolent drug crimes that would have been dealt with through medical intervention and rehabilitation forty years ago. The enslavement of Africans in the American south after the Civil War and the racist practices of Jim Crow laws have now been replaced by mass incarceration. After the gains of the Civil Rights movement of the 1960s, we have lost ground with racial practices of mass incarceration directed at poor African Americans and Latino/as who are viewed as cheap labor.[24]

Lest one think that people of color are imprisoned because they commit crimes more often than whites, consider the fact that whites use drugs at about the same rate as blacks, but blacks suffer incarceration while whites are less likely to be processed through the criminal justice system. The so-called "War on Drugs" and "law and order" give ideological support for the incarceration of African Americans as thinly veiled racist rhetoric for the "War on Blacks." One of the system links that support these racial practices is that people of color are specifically targeted by police who make racially biased decisions as to whom to stop in a traffic violation or other entry points. The recent litany of police shootings of black men on the pretense of traffic stops and alleged criminal activity is the first step in the mass-incarceration process in part because the black man has been stereotyped as the violent criminal even though the evidence does not support this image.[25]

To make matters worse, educational institutions are used to support racial mass incarceration in what has been called the "cradle-to-prison pipeline" and "schoolhouse-to-jailhouse."[26] Black children are socialized at a very young age to prepare for prison life. Children of color are derailed from academic and vocational careers and redirected to prison through explicit and implicit racist practices. Nearly one half of all black youths do

23. *Prison industrial complex* is a term coined by David, "Hell Factory in the Field," 229; also Davis, *The Prison Industrial Complex*; on the costs of mass incarceration and the manner in which corporations are profiting, see the collection of essays in Herival and Wright, *Prison Profiteers*; also, Pettit, *Invisible Men*, 13.

24. Alexander, *The New Jim Crow*, 102–5.

25. Mauer, *Race to Incarcerate*, 118–41.

26. Levad, *Redeeming a Prison Society*, 170–76.

not graduate high school with their classmates. Fourteen percent of African American youth drop out of school, 46 percent are detained in juvenile justice facilities, and 58 percent of all black juvenile offenders are sent to adult prisons even though they make up only 15 percent of the population.[27] Black youths are targeted and socialized for prison through strict school punishment under so-called "zero-tolerance policies" and being labeled with disabilities that direct them on paths with severe disadvantages. Black children are nearly twice as likely to be labeled as "learning disabled" or "emotionally disturbed" as white children and three to four times more likely to be labeled as mentally disabled.[28] Black boys make up 11 percent of the student population, but 35 percent of those are suspended, and 44 percent of those are expelled. African American children are disciplined more frequently and severely than their white peers and for less serious violations that are often based on subjective reasoning for issues such as disrespect, disruption, excessive noise, perceived threats, and loitering.[29] Children of color are refracted through stereotypes that define African Americans as more violent and dangerous; and the misbehavior or misdeeds of black children are not perceived as childlike (as with white children), but they are "adultified" as being willfully bad.[30] Laura Crystal argues, "What the cradle-to-prison pipeline really tries to holistically critique is a broad range of structural conditions under which extraordinary family dysfunction and a route to nowhere makes logical sense. It rails against macroeconomic policies and practices like those that inadequately regulate preventative health care, quality education, affordable housing, and living wage as flat-out wrong and gravely dangerous."[31] It does not suffice to say that somehow children of color are biologically or culturally prone to criminal behavior even though some pundits argue this way. Discriminatory practices socialize young black children for a life in prison through disciplinary practices and labeling.

Mass incarceration on the whole is a systemic process that needs to be critiqued and dismantled. No other advanced nation systematically imprisons and devalues its population the way that the U.S. does. The linking together of mass incarceration systems discriminates against African

27. Laura, *Being Bad*, 15; see also Holzman, *The Chains of Black America*, 39–40.
28. Laura, *Being Bad*, 19–20.
29. Ibid., 17.
30. Ibid., 18.
31. Ibid., 32.

Americans and Hispanics who are more likely to suffer the consequences even though whites commit similar crimes at about the same rate. Given these discriminatory practices, the Christian moral response should be one of resistance following in the prophetic tradition of Jesus and his disciples, who resisted Roman occupation. Mass incarceration is a social issue requiring a public response in which the dehumanizing practices are identified and resisted in order to change the systems to reflect fairness and true justice. Just as the Civil Rights movement of the 1960s led by Martin Luther King Jr. actively resisted the Jim Crow policies and practices of racial discrimination, so too a new movement of social resistance is needed to change the morally bankrupt practice of mass incarceration.[32] Active resistance is a moral response to injustices and inequalities.

CONCLUSION

Social ethics has a long history in Christianity. Postcolonial and empire studies have demonstrated that the life of Jesus and the meaning of the New Testament capture a history and narrative of social resistance to the brutal subjugation of Roman rule. If one has an ear to hear, the rhetorical codes and hidden transcript of Roman resistance not only support the ethic of social justice, but speak to issues of social justice today. Social justice discerns the disparities between the social orders and structures that dehumanize the vision of what *ought* to be in order to uphold the dignity in all human beings. Mass incarceration in the U.S. is a crisis that has subjugated poor African Americans and Latinos/as in a way that dehumanizes and impoverishes. The consequences of mass incarceration are that it has relegated people of color to an underclass in society through linked systems that target and dehumanize blacks and browns for nonviolent crimes that did not exist forty years ago. The linked systems of criminal justice have taken a medical issue in drug use and addiction, criminalized it, and then used this crime to incarcerate for longer periods of time, create barriers for improving the lives of the felons and their families, and even disenfranchise them. The irony is that whites are involved in drug use and addiction at the same rates, but they are not targeted, charged, or incarcerated in the same way or at the same rate. Social ethics demands that the racist policies and practices be dismantled so that people of color are afforded their God-given

---

32. Alexander, *The New Jim Crow*, 245–48.

dignity and rights. Active resistance is a means to foment change to bring about a more just society that reflects the image of God in all people.

ADDITIONAL RESOURCES

1. Learn more about a Christian response to the problem of mass incarceration by reading the "Starter Kit" available at http://nationalcouncilofchurches.us/images/CEEFFLD_2015_SKTL_MI.pdf.
2. Watch videos about the needs for social reform in the U.S. justice system at http://www.sentencingproject.org/template/page.cfm?id=187 and http://tedxtalks.ted.com/video/The-future-of-race-in-America-M.

DISCUSSION QUESTIONS

1. How does thinking about the Roman occupation add to our understanding of Christian morality?
2. How does Horsley's ideas of "official" and "hidden" transcripts help us evaluate cultural attitudes toward women and the children of illegal immigrants?
3. What are the components of "mass incarceration"?
4. Why is mass incarceration a moral issue in need of a Christian response?

REFERENCES

Alexander, Michelle. *The New Jim Crow: Mass Incarceration in the Age of Colorblindness.* New York: New, 2010.
Brueggemann, Walter. *The Prophetic Imagination.* Philadelphia: Fortress, 1978.
Crokett, Joseph V., ed. "Starter Kit for Teaching and Learning about Mass Incarceration." Washington, DC: National Council of Churches in Christ USA, 2015, http://nationalcouncilofchurches.us/images/CEEFFLD_2015_SKTL_MI.pdf (accessed June 27, 2016).
David, Mike. "Hell Factory in the Field: A Prison Industrial Complex." *The Nation* (February 20, 1995) 229.
Davis, Angela. *The Prison Industrial Complex.* Oakland: AK, 2001. CD-ROM.
Garland, David. "Introduction: The Meaning of Mass Incarceration." In *Mass Imprisonment: Social Causes and Consequences*, edited by David Garland, 1–3. Thousand Oaks, CA: Sage, 2001.

Herival, Tara, and Paul Wright, eds. *Prison Profiteers: Who Makes Money from Mass Incarceration?* New York: New, 2007.

Holzman, Michael. *The Chains of Black America: The Hammer of the Police, The Anvil of Schools.* Briarcliff Manor, NY: Chelmsford, 2014.

Horsley, Richard A. "Introduction." In *Paul and Empire: Religion and Power in Roman Imperial Society*, edited by Richard A. Horsley, 88–95. Harrisburg, PA: Trinity, 1997.

———. *Jesus and Empire: The Kingdom of God and the New World Disorder.* Minneapolis: Augsburg, 2003.

———. *Religion and the Empire: People, Power, and the Life of the Spirit.* Minneapolis: Fortress, 2003.

Laura, Crystal T. *Being Bad: My Baby Brother and the School-to-Prison Pipeline.* New York: Teachers College, 2014.

Levad, Amy. *Redeeming a Prison Society: A Liturgical and Sacramental Response to Mass Incarceration.* Minneapolis: Fortress, 2014.

Mauer, Marc. *Race to Incarcerate: The Sentencing Project.* New York: New, 1999.

McKnight, Scot, and Joseph B. Modica, eds. *Jesus Is Lord Caesar Is Not: Evaluating Empire in New Testament Studies.* Downers Grove, IL: IVP Academic, 2013.

Pettit, Beckey. *Invisible Men: Mass Incarceration and the Myth of Black Progress.* New York: Sage, 2012.

The Sentencing Project. 2016. http://www.sentencingproject.org/template/page.cfm?id=122. Accessed June 16, 2016.

Simon, Jonathan. *Mass Incarceration on Trial: A Remarkable Court Decision and the Future about Prisons in America.* New York: New, 2014.

Wacquant, Loïc. "When Ghetto and Prison Meet and Mesh." In *Mass Incarceration: Social Causes and Consequences*, edited by David Garland. Thousand Oaks, CA: Sage, 2001.

Wright, N. T. *The Challenge of Jesus: Rediscovering Who Jesus Is and Was.* Downers Grove, IL: IVP Academic, 1999.

PART TWO

How Christians Analyze and Respond to Contemporary Moral Issues

6

An Introduction to the Application of Christian Morality

Brandon Schmidly

and

Geoffrey W. Sutton

At that time Jesus went through the grainfields on the Sabbath. His disciples were hungry and began to pick some heads of grain and eat them. When the Pharisees saw this, they said to him, "Look! Your disciples are doing what is unlawful on the Sabbath."

He answered, "Haven't you read what David did when he and his companions were hungry? He entered the house of God, and he and his companions ate the consecrated bread—which was not lawful for them to do, but only for the priests. Or haven't you read in the Law that the priests on Sabbath duty in the temple desecrate the Sabbath and yet are innocent? I tell you that something greater than the temple is here. If you had known what these words mean, 'I desire mercy, not sacrifice,' you would not have condemned the innocent. For the Son of Man is Lord of the Sabbath."

Matthew 12:1–8 (NIV)

CHRISTIAN MORALITY—PART TWO

FROM FOUNDATION TO APPLICATION

IN THIS INTERACTION RECOUNTED in the book of Matthew Jesus highlights a common shortcoming in moral practice. The Pharisees surely knew the story of David's men and surely knew of the principle in the book of Hosea that Jesus referenced. The failure of the Pharisees, in part, is that their awareness of the principle did not translate into an accurate application in their actions. As a result, they were imposing *moral* constraints on society that were not consistent with true scriptural morality.

Genuine morality requires at least two things: understanding morality and being moral. If someone understands that an action is wrong but does not act accordingly, that person is immoral. At the same time, if someone does what is right but does not know that it is right, the person is not immoral but also not moral. Such a person is accidentally doing what is right.

These two distinct aspects of morality distinguish the preceding chapters from what follows. The preceding chapters 2, 3, 4, and 5 were written from the foundational disciplines of morality: respectively, philosophy, psychology, sociology, and theology. Chapter 2 introduced moral reasoning and demonstrated a philosophical process for reaching conclusions about morality. Chapter 3 introduced an approach to morality from the behavioral sciences and presented six factors (the SCOPES model) that influence how we act as well as six categories of reasons people use when describing behavior as either moral or immoral. In chapter 4, a sociological analysis revealed ways that individuals and society impact each other and the power of social context on people's attitudes. And in chapter 5, a contemporary theological interpretation of the New Testament was presented and, as a bridge to part 2, this interpretation was applied to a current moral issue in the United States.

In the following chapters, the reader has opportunity to take these foundational concepts into topics of applied ethics. Applied ethics is the field of ethics that evaluates real situations (or situation types) and engages in moral decision-making at that level. Applied ethics is the type of moral decision-making that Christians engage on a daily basis. When most people feel the weight of the ethical dilemma, it is concerning questions like "what should I say to this person?"; "Should I be involved in this cause?"; "Should I go on this business trip with my co-worker of the opposite sex?"; "How should I vote on this ballot measure regarding homosexuality?"; "Given my circumstances, should I get a divorce?"; "Given my young daughter's circumstances, is it ok for her to have an abortion?"

AN INTRODUCTION TO THE APPLICATION OF CHRISTIAN MORALITY

While you may have already formed a quick answer to these questions in your mind, it is not difficult to imagine specific circumstances in which these decisions become very difficult. When we face these sorts of issues, we've sometimes been told to ask ourselves, "What would Jesus do?"[1] This question provides a way to help us move from foundational principles to applied decisions. But how would Jesus make applied moral decisions? Did he "just know" the right thing to do? Did he just go with his gut? Perhaps, but the passage above shows that Jesus used moral principles as reasons for making some (perhaps all) of his applied moral judgements. Many people act as if their "gut" is the ultimate arbiter of moral decision-making, but it should be obvious that such an approach can lead to many poor decisions and actions. If we think about why it is helpful to ask about what Jesus would do, it is probably because we believe that Jesus acted according to correct moral principles, and by reflecting on his character, we are more likely to make applied decisions on the basis of correct moral principles.

Principles are perhaps the most useful tool in ethics. Principles are general truths that help clarify specific issues. In the moment of moral decision-making, sometimes there is not enough time to reflect thoroughly and clearly on the situation. In such cases, the best we can do is depend upon principles. However, moral principles are only trustworthy if they have sufficient justification. Many people who are indecisive are so because of a lack of principles. Either indecisiveness or poorly constructed principles can lead to immoral actions.

Principles are not something you can simply buy at the store. You might be able to buy a book containing moral principles, but you won't be driven by them unless you sincerely think they are true. And you can't apply them unless you understand them. These are the two challenges of principles. One, "how do I determine which principles to accept?" In other words, what principles are true? This question should be worked out through the foundational considerations from the previous chapters. The second challenge is "how do I apply my accepted moral principles to real-world decisions?" The following chapters are intended to provide examples of moral decision-making regarding specific issues.

Even if there are four primary foundational disciplines of study for morality, people in every discipline face moral dilemmas that require decisions. In keeping with the interdisciplinary approach of the book, the following chapters will engage applied topics in a variety of disciplines.

1. Sheldon, *In His Steps*.

CHRISTIAN MORALITY—PART TWO

WHAT WILL YOU FIND IN PART 2?

Chapter 7: Using Philosophy to Think about Abortion by Brandon Schmidly

Brandon Schmidly engages the abortion conversation by providing clarity on the relevant concepts when considering the moral issues of abortion. He discusses the nature of personhood and evaluates arguments for when the rights of persons begin. He then presents and evaluates arguments based on the rights of the mother, potentiality, and our responsibilities to help those in need.

There are many moral issues that involve an understanding of human rights and human life. Closely related to the abortion issue is the matter of birth control. Thinking about human rights and life is also important to decisions about ending lives sustained by medical technology, capital punishment, and taking the lives of others in self-defense. We hope this chapter helps you think about a Christian perspective on human rights and life.

Chapter 8: Sexual Minorities, Same-Sex Marriage, and Christian Morality by Geoffrey W. Sutton

Geoff Sutton helps the reader think through the issues of sexual identity and same-sex relationships. He explains the ways that people talk about sexuality. He then applies the SCOPES model, outlined in chapter 3, to clarify moral issues related specifically to sexual identity and same-sex relationships. He also explains how different Christians view these issues. Sutton then considers several biblical passages relevant to the topic, and he closes with suggestions for Christians making moral judgments on related issues, such as same-sex marriage.

We hope the analysis of same-sex marriage provides you with an example of how to think about a topic that often involves arguments presented with strong emotions. First, Christians are encouraged to understand the biblical texts they are using to support a Christian perspective. Second, readers need to understand facts about human nature before offering unsupported opinions about sexuality. Third, it is vital to understand the basis for a particular argument. That is, are Christians providing carefully reasoned moral arguments consistent with Scripture, or are their reasons more related to emotional factors, such as those derived from research on the emotion of disgust?

Chapter 9: A Woman's Place: Perspectives on Gender Equality by Ruth Burgess

Ruth Burgess makes the case that gender inequality is a human rights problem on a global scale. She highlights specific areas of inequality and how they affect women. She then argues that Christians should be advocates who engage in efforts to bring about gender equality in the specific social contexts of religion, politics, and socioeconomic venues.

As you work through Burgess's chapter, we encourage you to consider what it means to treat men and women as equals. For example, is it morally right to exclude women from certain roles in Christian ministry? Second, consider the texts Burgess quotes. Notice she quotes from ancient sources that have not been a part of most Christian Bibles (e.g., *Gospel of Mary*). How does this use of ancient texts influence your thinking about the treatment of women? Finally, we encourage you to evaluate Burgess, suggestions on how to think about gender equality. For example, do you find her approach helpful? Does her approach help you think about matters of equality in other aspects of society, such as the equal treatment of minorities?

Chapter 10: Tensions and Challenges: Christian Morality and Sex Education by April Montoya and Shonna Crawford

April Montoya and Shonna Crawford make a case for how Christians in the field of education should approach the topic of sex education. They highlight the need for sex education in schools, and they highlight some of the moral concerns related to teaching sex education. They then explain two historical approaches that have been used in the field of education, noting the benefits and challenges of each. Then they propose a way forward that involves the six essential components of values, relationships, media literacy, abstinence, risks, and contraceptives. They argue that a method that involves these components is something that Christian educators can support.

Although this chapter is clearly about sex education, we encourage you to think broadly about the importance of a Christian framework in teaching anyone anything in which the content of what is taught can vary depending on whether the subject is taught from a Christian, secular, or other religious perspective. We also encourage you to notice how the authors integrate references to Scripture with facts about sexuality and relationships.

Chapter 11: Morality in Local and Global Perspectives by Paul W. Lewis

Paul Lewis, former foreign missionary, presents the moral challenges that arise in cross-cultural contexts. He engages the reader with clear examples of how cultural differences can be the cause of specific challenges in behavior and in understanding what it means to be a Christian. He presents three prominent cultural perspectives on religious experiences and biblical interpretation. Lewis then makes a case for the need of Christians to be cross-culturally, transculturally, and counter-culturally aware.

Lewis' chapter offers us an example of thinking clearly about our understanding of morality when we judge the behavior of other Christians to be immoral. In the chapter, we learn that large groups of Christians in one nation can have a different view of right conduct than do Christians from another national culture. Lewis is not arguing for moral relativism, but he does encourage us to think carefully about the difference between Christian principles and the way those principles are expressed in different cultures.

REFLECTIONS

Similar to the chapters in part 1, the following chapters will conclude with discussion questions and additional references to give the reader material for going deeper into the specific topic. It is the authors' hope that these chapters will both provide good examples of Christians engaging moral issues from various walks of life as well as inspire you to do the same. The book will close with some overall reflections from the authors.

7

Using Philosophy to Think About Abortion

BRANDON SCHMIDLY

"What is written in the law? . . . Love your neighbor as yourself . . . Do this and you will live."

Luke 10:26–28 (NIV)

IN JAMAICA, 2010, HUGO was walking down the street when he noticed a woman being attacked. He jumped in to rescue the woman and was stabbed several times in the chest. The attacker ran, and as Hugo attempted to chase, he fell to the ground unable to continue running. Over the next several minutes, as many as twenty-five people walked by Hugo. Some looked closely enough to know that something terrible had happened. None helped. This entire incident was captured on surveillance video.[1] Many who watch this video are shocked, outraged. How could people just walk by? Perhaps they thought he was already dead. But if they knew he could be saved, weren't they wrong in walking away?

Does this case say anything about the abortion debate? Some will immediately say no. But by the end of the chapter I will revisit a case like this. This chapter is not intended to condemn anyone who has had an abortion. One thing is sure: there are many factors to consider, and the public

1. Livingston, Doyle, and Mangan, "Stabbed Hero Dies."

discourse is so loud and so toxic that it is not surprising many have no clear sense of what is morally right when it comes to abortion. However, rather than walk away from this messy topic, Christians should be all the more compelled to search for truth and clarity regarding abortion.

INTRODUCTION

Abortion is one of the most controversial issues. This is, in part, because it is tied to so many other areas of passionate feelings such as sex, politics, power, money, guilt, life, and death. In this chapter, let's try, as best as possible, to consider the morality of abortion in and of itself. Even when we do that, we find a conflict of two of our most deeply held values, life and liberty.

This chapter will focus on the question, "Is abortion ever morally permissible?" which is distinct from the question, "Should abortion ever be legal?"[2] The answer to the second question does not necessarily follow from the first. There are some activities, say, laziness, which may not be moral even though there is good reason to not criminalize it. However, in many ways, our answer to the second will follow our answer to the first. For although there is a conceptual distinction between the moral and legal question, in the case of abortion they are likely going to be more closely tied together than in other topics. For if it is determined that abortion is immoral, it will likely be for reasons that demand legal intervention (e.g., because it destroys an innocent life). As such, it is odd that so many people say they oppose abortion but do not think it should be illegal.

In what follows, I will first clarify relevant concepts in the abortion conversation. I will then consider arguments for the conclusion that abortion is not morally permissible. I will then consider the most prominent argument for the permissibility of abortion. Finally, I will argue that the argument for the permissibility of abortion fails. It will be up to you to consider whether the counterargument succeeds.

A BIBLICAL CASE

Of course, the concept of an abortion was not part of the ancient world. As such, we cannot look to scripture and expect to find explicit permission or

2. See Gert, "The Definition of Morality."

prohibition regarding abortion. While murder is explicitly forbidden in the Ten Commandments, we cannot directly apply that to abortion without making controversial assumptions about the status of the fetus, namely that the fetus is a person with rights.[3]

Contemporary Christians have regularly been counted among the pro-life movement, and often Christians cite specific scriptural passages as providing principled support for the pro-life position. Consider Jeremiah 1:5 where God says, "Before I formed you in the womb I knew you, and before you were born I set you apart."[4] Another is Psalm 139:13, which states, "you knit me together in my mother's womb."[5] Another is Luke chapter 1, in which we read that when Mary, was pregnant with Jesus, she visited Elizabeth, who was pregnant with John the Baptist. When Mary entered the room, John leapt in Elizabeth's womb.[6]

Do these passages imply a pro-life position? Perhaps. The first two passages are poetic, the third is narrative, and each clearly places value, of some sort, on what is happening in the womb. How strong is that value? Is it strong enough to imply that the fetus has the full rights of a person and that abortion is impermissible? The argument many make is that both Jeremiah and David are stating that God knew them in the womb; therefore, they began to exist, as a person, before they were born. Perhaps this is correct; however, we often hear phrases like, "While he was on the cross, I was on his mind."[7] This means that many believe God is able to know us, in some sense, even before we exist. And such a possibility weakens the pro-life inference made from the passages cited.

Certainly stronger biblical cases can be made, and there are stronger objections than what was just discussed. Even if stronger cases are available, many Christians are unaware of them, and they base their pro-life position on something as weak as the verses mentioned above. As such, many who are not pro-life are not persuaded by the "biblical case" made by many Christians. And, almost certainly, a pro-life advocate who does not accept the authority of Scripture will not be moved by a biblical case against abortion.

3. This will be discussed later in the chapter.
4. Jer 1:5 (NIV).
5. Ps 139:13 (NIV).
6. For a much more developed presentation of a case from Scripture, see Rae, *Moral Choices*.
7. From the song by the same name, written by Bill and Gloria Gaither.

I believe, however, that many Christians are firmly convinced that the pro-life position is consistent with a Christian worldview, even if they cannot cite Scripture that explicitly makes this implication. In these instances, Christians should be willing to consider evidence and arguments from other disciplines, such as philosophy and science, to see if there are clear cases for a pro-life position, even if the basic assumptions do not include scriptural references.

IS IT EVER MORALLY PERMISSIBLE?

There is a spectrum of positions that one can take on the continuum of the permissibility question. On one end of the spectrum is the view that abortion is never permissible. The other end is the view that it is always permissible. In between the extremes are views that hold abortion is permissible in some circumstances and not in others. Even among these views, sometimes the relevant circumstances are in the womb (e.g., second trimester, viability, heartbeat), and sometimes the relevant circumstances are external (e.g., rape, incest, age of the mother).

Think for a moment about the variety of things that affect one's answer to the question, "Is abortion permissible?" Some questions must be answered by biologists: When is a fetus viable? When can a fetus feel pain? Many people think that the only relevant issue is when life begins. But notice, even if we settled that question, it does not end the discussion. For, even if everyone agrees that there is a life in the womb; one could argue that a woman's liberties can outweigh the value of her child's life. Or, even if we agree a fetus is not a person, one could argue that abortion is impermissible because of the potential life that exists, or because of the rights of the biological father, or because of the effect on society (etc.). It would be impossible, in a single chapter, to address all of the relevant questions in such a way that it settles the abortion conversation. The goal of this chapter is to demonstrate how philosophers and ethicists work through an issue to reach conclusions, or reasonable answers, to relevant questions.

CLARIFYING RELEVANT CONCEPTS

Abortion

There are several sub-questions that one must consider when considering whether abortion is permissible. For instance, is the developing fetus a life? How do you weigh the rights of the mother against the rights of her unborn child? Does it matter how the fetus came to exist? If abortion is wrong, is it the type of wrong that can be prevented by legal force? And there are many more questions. Like most controversial topics, this one is complex, and one chapter cannot cover it all. But let's at least get off to a good start and begin with a basic question, "What is abortion?"

In a clear-minded moral discussion, we should be careful to avoid terms that emotionally skew the conversation to one side or the other. When emotionally charged terms are used, the philosophical conversation ends because one side will not agree to the initial definitions. For instance, one might define the being in the womb as a "child," or we might define it as "tissue." Either definition will skew the argument. So, how can we define abortion? At a minimum, abortion is the premature ending of a pregnancy. Abortion (in the sense that most people care about) is also intentional and externally caused. A pregnancy is the developmental process of egg-zygote-embryo-fetus-infant. Many people use the term *fetus* as a catch-all term for the developing being. So I think everyone can agree that abortion is the intentional, externally caused cessation of the development of a fetus.

Rights and Persons

Because the abortion conversation significantly involves a discussion of rights (e.g., rights of the mother, rights of the unborn, rights of the father), we will lean heavily on the rights-based concepts that were discussed in chapter 2. So in this chapter we will assume a basic rights framework. People have rights. Fully autonomous human beings are full right-holders. In general, rights protect choices, but, in some cases, rights protect interests. Things that have no choices or interests (e.g. rocks) do not have rights. Persons (i.e., beings with rights) must begin to exist, and most persons are not full right-holders until they are fully autonomous adults. Thus, there is a continuum along which we can plot a right-holder from basic human rights to full rights of autonomy (self-governance).

Nearly everyone agrees that it is *prima facie* wrong to intentionally terminate a person's life (we call it murder).[8] And the reason it is wrong is that it violates a fundamental right, the right to life. Also, most agree that it is prima facie *not* wrong to prevent a person's life from beginning; we call it contraception. However, since there is debate about when personhood specifically begins, it is an open question as to whether abortion is contraception or murder. Since ending an innocent life becomes (prima facie) murder once a person exists, reaching a conclusion regarding the beginning of personhood would contribute substantially to the abortion debate.[9]

Let's address the concept of personhood. *Person* has become the term by which political philosophers refer to a being with rights, specifically the rights we attribute to normal human beings. We use the word *personhood* instead of *life* because, although many things are alive (plants, bugs, etc.), a person has rights. The term *person* should also not be conflated with the term *human being*. Some human beings do not have rights (e.g., a corpse). The term *human being* picks out a biological category of beings. Furthermore, it is theoretically possible that nonhumans could be persons. For instance, if an alien race was discovered that could think, reason, and feel as we do, then we would likely think of the aliens as persons.

The entity in the womb is clearly alive in a biological sense. Furthermore, it is clearly a human being. But is there a person (a thing with rights) in the womb? If the answer is no, then abortion will only be impermissible if it violates the rights of someone other than the being in the womb. If the answer is yes, then it will be difficult to argue for the permissibility of abortion.[10]

---

8. Philosophers use the term *prima facie* (the Latin phrase for "on the face") to discuss things as they are, without outside considerations. So, for instance, the act of ceasing your biological development (i.e., killing you) is wrong on its face. But given other considerations, like the fact that you are threatening to kill me, it may be *all-things-considered* not wrong. See Ross, *The Right and the Good*.

9. See the discussion of personhood in chapter 2. See also Griffin, *On Human Rights*; and Kant, *Groundwork*. Some frame the rights issue in abortion as a matter of moral status. See Jaworska, "Caring."

10. Although Thomson's argument, presented later in this chapter, will do just that.

ARGUMENTS FROM PERSONHOOD

An argument from personhood can be made by either the pro-life or pro-choice position, depending on when one can determine personhood to begin. There are two approaches to answering the question, "Is the fetus a person?" The first is less a question of abortion and more a question of the conditions of personhood. If we can determine the necessary and sufficient conditions for personhood, we would then only need to ask whether, and when, the developing fetus acquires those features.

This task, however, is more difficult than it may seem. What measurable conditions make you a person (right-holder)? Is it the fact that you are sentient (i.e., feel things like pain)? If you ceased to be sentient, would you cease to be a person? Is it the fact that you are self-aware? Perhaps, but do you cease to be a person while you're asleep? Is it the fact that you are, biologically, a human being? Perhaps, but if we could change your biology (e.g., through robotic limbs) would you cease to be a person, or be less of a person? Would you cease to have rights?

When we attempt to answer the question regarding conditions of personhood, we run into the problem of separation. The problem of separation occurs in attempts to provide necessary and sufficient conditions. Specifically, when every proposed condition, or set of conditions, has a clear counterexample.

Given the difficulty of specifying the conditions of personhood, we can make progress in the abortion discussion through a process of elimination. Logicians call this argument type a disjunctive syllogism. In a disjunctive syllogism, you exhaust the possibilities in a disjunctive statement (either A is true, or B, or C). Then you eliminate possibilities (B is false). And you conclude what is left (Therefore, either A or C).

Given that a fertilized egg will become a person at some point, what are the most plausible beginning options? Here are some that are often considered: fertilization, when brain activity is present, when the heart starts beating, sentience, quickening, viability, or birth.[11] Can any of these options be eliminated? Viability seems to be problematic. With new technology, more and more premature births result in healthy children. So viability is different today than it was twenty years ago. However, personhood is surely

---

11. This list, obviously, does not exhaust all of the possibilities. However, these are the most commonly discussed. Some ethicists, most notably Peter Singer, have argued for some time after birth.

not changeable based on technology. So it seems that viability can be eliminated as an option.

You might be thinking, "Hold on! Perhaps viability can be modified to work." Perhaps we could modify the viability option to be something like "unassisted viability"; that is, viable without the intervention of non-natural technology. In this case, even though we can successfully maintain a fetus outside the womb, until it is viable on its own, it is not a person. This modification, however, seems to have some implications that are difficult to accept. First, it would imply that a prematurely born fetus who is kept alive by machines has no rights. And it seems clear that, were someone to harm a prematurely born child, they would be doing something wrong. And the wrong is not merely against the parents or society, but the child. So, given that the unassisted viability condition has this implication, and the implication is false, the unassisted viability option would also be false.

Birth, as a starting point for personhood, also seems problematic. When a birth occurs, what is relevantly different from the moment before birth such that the being is now a person and wasn't before? It seems the only difference is that the body of the child is not attached to the mother's body. Is that relevant? Imagine that a child could be a normal infant without detaching from the mother's body. Let's say, hypothetically, that the child grows for two years this way, learning to talk, walk, etc., but all the while attached with the umbilical cord. Would we say that personhood has not begun simply because the bodies are still attached? If the answer is "no," as I think it is, then the birth process does not provide a relevant change to mark the beginning of personhood.

The other intermediate options (brain activity, heartbeat, sentience, etc.) are not so obviously bad, but all have problems as well, and many philosophers think there is a good reason to eliminate each of them as plausible beginning points for personhood. This would leave us with fertilization (or conception) as the last standing option for when personhood begins. While this is the conclusion most conservative Christians wish to reach, the "conception" option is not without problems. For one, at conception, there is a single cell, and it is intuitively strange to say that a single cell is a person. What is present that would make the single cell a person? Some appeal to the fact that it has a unique DNA. But why think that a distinct DNA makes you a person? Consider, hypothetically, if we discovered aliens that had no DNA at all, yet they acted like us. Wouldn't we still think that it would be wrong to torture and kill them? In other words, we would assume they have rights, and, thus, are persons. So, a distinct DNA is not conceptually *necessary* for personhood. Furthermore, a corpse has a distinct DNA, yet we think that personhood ends at death. So, a distinct DNA is not *sufficient* for personhood. If that evaluation is correct, then it is still unclear why conception produces a morally relevant change that results in personhood. Even granting this concern, conception may be the least problematic of the possible options. If so, then it is the most rational conclusion for when personhood begins.

PROBABILITY AND POTENTIALITY ARGUMENTS

Given the discussion in the previous section, some people remain agnostic with regard to when personhood begins. In other words, they conclude that it is something we just cannot know. However, even when something is not knowable, it is reasonable to ask, "If we don't know, what do we do?" From here, one of the pro-life arguments calls for society to err on the side of caution. The idea is something like this: if there is a chance that a fetus is a person, the moral action is to not abort.

This sort of argument is based on probability. Although probability-based arguments are weaker than deductively valid arguments, they are more common to how we live day-to-day. Consider an example about making a decision to drive to work. There are several probabilities you could consider. If you go, there are possible negatives, such as dying in a car accident, and there are possible positives, such as earning a day's wage. If you thought that the negatives were sufficiently probable, you wouldn't go. But most of us decide to go to work because the probability of realizing the positive outcome is sufficiently high, and the probability of realizing a negative outcome is sufficiently low. As such, there is a reasonable conclusion even in a case of uncertainty. Can a similar approach be used in the abortion conversation? John Noonan offers such an argument.

Noonan's argument from probability is an analogy, and it goes as follows. Consider someone who has a new rifle and is out in the woods trying it out. At one point, the new gun owner aims to shoot into a bush. Just before the trigger is pulled, the gun owner sees the bush rustle and wonders if there is a person in the bush. From here, the probabilities will determine whether the gun owner is morally permitted to shoot. If the probability of there not being a person is, say, two hundred thousand to one, then it is morally permissible to shoot.[12] However, if the probability is four out of five, then it is morally wrong to shoot. Noonan then states that, for any given fetus, there is a four out of five probability that, if left alone, it will become a person. From this analogy, Noonan concludes that it is morally impermissible to abort a fetus.

Does Noonan's analogy succeed? Two relevant issues seem to be present in the gunman scenario. One problem with Noonan's analogy is the difference between the uses of probability. In the case of the being in the bush, the thing is currently either a person or not (100 percent). What is a matter of probability is our belief about the being in the bush, and the likelihood of a person being there. His four-out-of-five statistic about the fetus has to do with what will be, not what currently is. However, we could perhaps adjust the analogy to be useful and apply probability to our discussion regarding personhood. In other words, even in a case of uncertainty about when personhood begins, we can assess the probability of personhood having begun, even if there is doubt. In this case, we can consider the options from before (conception, heartbeat, birth), and if we conclude that, say, there is a 75 percent chance that personhood begins sometime while the fetus is in the womb, then we may conclude that abortion (at least some types of abortion) are wrong, in spite of our uncertainty.

Noonan's appeal to the fact that four out of five fetuses will become people is more of an appeal to potentiality. Surely everyone can agree that there is, at least, a potential person in the womb. Does potentiality create a moral obligation? In some cases it does. When people are injured, the courts will often make awards on the basis of the potential earnings of the person. In other words, the injured has a right to those earnings, even though they had not yet been realized. In other cases, potentiality is limited. A president-elect does not have the right to make presidential decisions based on a nearly certain potentiality that he/she will be president. Which type of scenario more accurately fits the case of a fetus? Even if we grant that a fetus is not a person, does the fact that a potential person exists create rights for the potential person in a fetal state?[13]

---

12. The actual number here is not the issue. If you would rather make it one million to one, that's fine. The point will still be the same.

13. Feinberg offers a well-known account on the basis of potentiality.

USING PHILOSOPHY TO THINK ABOUT ABORTION

FROM PERSONHOOD TO THE RIGHTS OF THE MOTHER

Many people argue over the personhood of the fetus as if answering that question concludes the abortion debate. Judith Jarvis Thomson presents a series of pro-choice arguments on the basis of the rights of the biological mother; we will consider her first argument. In this argument, she grants that a fetus is a person with a full right to life. She then asks, are there some instances where it is morally permissible to end a person's life?

Most people will grant that, in some cases, it is morally permissible to end a person's life. If you are being mortally threatened, most people think you can defend yourself using lethal force. In times of war, most (or many) people think it is permissible for a soldier to engage in lethal force. Perhaps in a case where one can lay down his or her life for a friend, a person may give permission for another to do something that will kill them but save others. If you agree that there are circumstances such that it is morally permissible to end a person's life, then we must ask, is that ever the case with abortion?

Thomson concludes that the answer is yes. She presents an analogy that is supposed to support her conclusion. Let's consider her analogy:

> But now let me ask you to imagine this. You wake up in the morning and find yourself back to back in bed with an unconscious violinist. A famous unconscious violinist. He has been found to have a fatal kidney ailment, and the Society of Music Lovers has canvassed all the available medical records and found that you alone have the right blood type to help. They have therefore kidnapped you, and last night the violinist's circulatory system was plugged into yours, so that your kidneys can be used to extract poisons from his blood as well as your own. The director of the hospital now tells you, "Look, we're sorry the Society of Music Lovers did this to you—we would never have permitted it if we had known. But still, they did it, and the violinist is now plugged into you. To unplug you would be to kill him. But never mind, it's only for nine months. By then he will have recovered from his ailment, and can safely be unplugged from you." Is it morally incumbent on you to accede to this situation? No doubt it would be very nice of you if you did, a great kindness. But do you have to accede to it? What if it were not nine months, but nine years? Or longer still? What if the director of the hospital says. "Tough luck. I agree. but now you've got to stay in bed, with the violinist plugged into you, for

the rest of your life. Because remember this. All persons have a right to life, and violinists are persons. Granted you have a right to decide what happens in and to your body, but a person's right to life outweighs your right to decide what happens in and to your body. So you cannot ever be unplugged from him."[14]

Thomson believes that it would be "outrageous" (i.e., immoral) to require someone to stay plugged into the violinist. It is clear, she believes, that your rights to personal autonomy, in this instance, are stronger than the violinist's right to life, thus it is not immoral for you to unplug from the violinist. Furthermore, given that factors of this story are relevantly analogous to some cases of abortion, in such cases it is not immoral for a mother to end the life of a fetus.

Some are initially dismissive of this analogy saying, "That hypothetical story is too silly." But let me caution you from such a response. First, notice that the laws of morality work even in hypothetical worlds. For instance, in the hypothetical world where I am wearing a different shirt, it is still wrong for me to injure you merely for fun. Second, no two cases in an analogy (even if neither are hypothetical) are exactly alike. Analogies, by definition, have differences (otherwise they are the same case). And the strength of the analogy depends on the relevance of the similarities and the irrelevance of the differences. So, if Thomson's case has enough relevant similarities (and few relevant dissimilarities), then the argument from analogy is cogent.

If we were to formalize her argument from analogy, it could look like this:

1. Some cases of abortion are relevantly analogous to the violinist case.
2. In the violinist case, it is permissible for you to detach from the violinist, which ends a life.
3. So, it is permissible (in analogous cases) for a mother to "detach" from a fetus, which ends a life.

There are two possible responses to Thomson. Some who disagree respond by denying premise two. Most who disagree respond by denying premise one.

Obviously premise one is not true in every instance of pregnancy. The violinist case would only be analogous to particular instances of pregnancy where the mother had no choice in the pregnancy, such as cases where

14. Thomson, "A Defense of Abortion," 47–66.

pregnancy results from rape. If we consider only those cases, is premise one true? Many think that it is. Let me challenge with a counterexample.

Let's consider an adaptation of a hypothetical case presented by Peter Singer. Suppose your route to work takes you by a shallow pond; you see a baby has just fallen into the pond and appears to be drowning. Obviously, someone else has done something greatly immoral (and likely criminal) by leaving a baby by the road, and, ultimately, that person is at fault. Still, there is no one else in sight, and unless you keep the baby alive, no one else will get there in time, and the child will die. However, before you jump into the water, you realize a few things. First, you are wearing new and expensive clothes. To save the child will cost you several hundred dollars in ruined clothing. Second, you will be late for work, and if you are, you will be passed up for this promotion cycle and your career will not advance for at least nine months.[15] Must you participate in keeping the child alive? Of course, "it would be very nice of you if you did, a great kindness." But do you have to jump in and keep the child alive? Do your rights over your own body and life make it permissible for you to walk away from the scene, knowing that the child will die? Many (perhaps most) would say no. And the story of Hugo, which began this chapter, suggests the same.

So, we have two seemingly relevant analogies to cases of pregnancy resulting from rape. In one case, the violinist case, the intuitions of many suggest we can unplug from the person and let him/her die. In the second case, the intuitions of many say that we cannot walk away without being morally culpable.

How, then, do we proceed? Do we give up and say, "I guess we will never know"? To do so is negligence. There is a possibility that people are dying from abortion, and that possibility deserves our best effort. This is the messy work of critical thought. It is likely that the answer will never be as clear as two plus two equals four. But that should not be expected. Few disciplines can produce answers with absolute clarity. Most areas of study require researchers to advance the most plausible answers possible, and the plausibility will be based on the evidence that can be provided and the ability to account for the counterevidence. In the case of moral philosophy, the evidence is our moral intuition and argumentation.

---

15. This case is an adaptation from Singer, "The Drowning Child." Singer uses a drowning child case as an analogy to motivate the conclusion that we should be helping the needy around the world. I have made adaptations to use it as a counterexample to Thomson.

So, which of the analogies above is more relevantly applicable to a case of abortion? This requires the process of reviewing analogies discussed in chapter 2. Both cases have similarities and differences to a case of pregnancy resulting from something like rape. Which situation has stronger relevant similarities and fewer (and weaker) relevant dissimilarities?

I think there are two relevant dissimilarities in the violinist case. First, the process of being attached to a violinist is (at least I would imagine) very different from being pregnant. Second, the fact that the violinist is an adult changes our intuition on the matter. Perhaps it should not make a difference; an innocent person is no less innocent for being older. However, we tend to think that competent adults should be responsible for themselves, and their troubles perhaps could have been avoided with better decision-making earlier in life. Notice that if you change the case from a violinist to a one-year-old child, you would probably find it even more distasteful to detach and let the person die. And in the drowning child case, we maintain that similarity, making the drowning child analogy stronger than the violinist analogy.

If this brief analysis is correct, then (assuming the fetus is a person) the moral responsibility to not walk away when we alone can save a life leads us to a pro-life position, even in the most extreme cases (e.g., rape). If, however, you find that you are still pro-choice with regard to abortion, it may be because you still hold that a fetus is likely not a person, and not because you think that abortion is a justified instance of letting a person die. This leads us back to the earlier arguments in this chapter about personhood.

In this chapter, I have presented some of the most notable considerations that arise in the abortion debate. When does personhood begin? Does probability or potentiality of personhood affect our decision-making? Do the liberty rights of mothers override the potential personhood of the child? I have briefly considered the arguments and now, as a reader, you should be able to more clearly articulate the conclusion you have reached.

ADDITIONAL RESOURCES

1. In 2015, Pope Francis changed the church's policy regarding forgiveness over having had an abortion (http://n.pr/1JuHTXe). Does such a change mark the beginning of a change in attitude among global Christianity regarding abortion?

2. In 2015, undercover videos were released that showed Planned Parenthood officials discussing the selling of fetal remains (http://n.pr/1OdLexj). Many found the videos emotionally disturbing but not as disturbing as the Kermit Gosnell case a few years earlier (http://wapo.st/1dnaFLH). What role, if any, does such evidence have in a rigorous discussion of the permissibility of abortion?

3. Passed in 1997, the Hyde Amendment prohibits federal funds from paying for abortion. This issue has played a significant role in political debates ranging from the Affordable Care Act (i.e., Obamacare) to funding Planned Parenthood. If abortion is legal, why not allow federal funds to subsidize the practice?

4. Should our governing documents provide a legal definition of personhood? There have been several attempts to do so (http://t.usnews.com/Z3ui3m?src=usn_tw via @usnews). Most have failed. Should this effort continue?

DISCUSSION QUESTIONS

1. Can someone be anti-abortion but pro-choice?
2. How confident can anyone be about when life (personhood) begins?
3. Do we have an obligation to allow potential persons to become actual persons?
4. Do the Scripture verses cited in this chapter make a strong case for a pro-life position? Explain.
5. Imagine you are a first-year female college student who has unintentionally become pregnant. In that mindset, is Thomson's analogy persuasive?

REFERENCES

Gert, Bernard. "The Definition of Morality." The Stanford Encyclopedia of Philosophy, edited by Edward N. Zalta, Fall 2015, http://plato.stanford.edu/archives/fall2015/entries/morality-definition (accessed June 27, 2016).
Feinberg, Joel. "Abortion." In *Matters of Life and Death*, edited by Tom Regan, 183–217. 2nd ed. Philadelphia: Temple University Press, 1986.
Griffin, James. *On Human Rights*. Oxford: Oxford University Press, 2008.
Jaworska, Agnieszka. "Caring and Full Moral Standing." *Ethics* 117 (2007) 460–97.

Kant, Immanuel. *The Groundwork for the Metaphysics of Morals*. Translated by Mary J. Gregor. 1785. Reprint, Cambridge: Cambridge University Press, 1998.

Livingston, Ikimulisa, John Doyle, and Dan Mangan. "Stabbed Hero Dies as More Than 20 People Stroll Past Him." *New York Post*, April 24, 2010.

Rae, Scott B. *Moral Choices: An Introduction to Ethics*. 3rd ed. Grand Rapids: Zondervan, 2009.

Ross, William D. *The Right and the Good*. Indianapolis: Hackett, 1988.

Charles M. Sheldon. *In His Steps*. Nashville: Broadman & Holman, 1986.

Singer, Peter. "The Drowning Child and the Expanding Circle." *New Internationalist* 289 (1997) 28–30.

Thomson, Judith Jarvis. "A Defense of Abortion." *Philosophy and Public Affairs* 1 (1971) 47–66.

8

Sexual Minorities, Same-Sex Marriage, and Christian Morality

Geoffrey W. Sutton

> *I used to teach a young girls group at church and was no longer allowed to teach the group. And I was encouraged to cut all ties with the girls. I have been asked not to return to a church unless I was willing to denounce my sexual orientation and admit that I was a sinner. Every time I see some people from the church I grew up in, they start preaching to me about my lifestyle.*[1]
>
> —Research Participant, Allman

CHAPTER OVERVIEW

THIS CHAPTER IS ABOUT the moral response of Christians toward people who identify as a sexual minority. Like the lesbian woman in the opening quote, many sexual minorities experience rejection from their churches. How is sexual identity different for sexual minorities? How do Christians interpret biblical texts to support their moral stance toward people with different sexual orientations? Why do some Christians support same-sex marriage when others do not? These questions form the broad outline for this chapter.

---

1. Quote from research participant in Allman, *Resilience*, 70.

For the first time in recorded history, several nations have officially recognized that a significant minority of men and women have different sexual identities and romantic interests than do the majority. As a part of that official recognition, several nations have legalized same-sex marriages. These changes have come about in the past few decades and represent a fast pace of social change compared to other social changes in human history. For example, for most of human history, people have been legally held as slaves, and most nations severely restricted the rights of women. Social activists worked for more than a century to end slavery, the unequal treatment of racial and ethnic minorities, and the minimal role of women. But changes to decriminalize same-sex activity, accord rights to LGBT persons, and approve same-sex marriage have occurred within the past few decades.

Christians have different views on the role of men and women in society and in the church. Most Christian traditions restrict the role of women in ministry, but this has changed in recent decades. When it comes to marriage, only a few Christian groups have changed their stance to marry same-sex couples. Christian leaders have explained why some forms of sexual activity are immoral and why a Christian marriage should only be between one man and one woman. In this chapter, I will attempt to clarify key moral issues related to sexual identity and same-sex marriage. To accomplish this goal, I will first explain some of the ways people talk about sexual identity and relationships that are not heterosexual. Second, I will refer to the SCOPES model outlined in chapter 3 to illustrate how key aspects of personal functioning can be different for sexual minorities. Third, I will show how Christians can use the six dimensions of moral psychology to appraise the way different Christians view the moral issues involved in sexual identity and same-sex marriage.

In concluding this overview, I will refer to the biblical texts that most people cite when discussing the morality of sexual activity other than sex within a marriage between one man and one woman. The first point most make comes from the creation account in Genesis chapters 1 and 2.[2] God created two sexes, male and female and joined them together in a blessed union. Jesus referred to these Genesis verses when he explained that God designed marriage as a permanent relationship.[3] A second point refers to

---

2. For example, *Theology of Sex*, 2.
3. Matt 19:4–6 (NIV).

the sins of the people at Sodom[4] and Gibeah.[5] Both stories refer to sexual assault and include references to desire for same-sex activity. Third, a law in Leviticus bans male-male sex.[6] Finally, the apostle Paul addressed the matter of sexual conduct and marriage[7] in a few places, but a passage from Rom 1:24–31 specifically mentions same-sex activity as wrong for both men and women. Jewish[8] and Christian[9] scholars have offered different opinions about the correct translation of the ancient words and phrases as well as the interpretation of these verses. Christian leaders also argue about how Hebrew laws and the teachings of Paul should guide contemporary Christians in how to live a moral life. I will address these issues further when analyzing different moral perspectives.

Finally, let me revise a phrase from chapter 3 suggesting how Christians form moral judgments related to same-sex marriage and related issues. Christian moral judgments about sex-related issues are based on four factors: (1) An interpretation of the biblical texts, (2) An understanding of human nature (e.g., SCOPES model), (3) a specific understanding of relevant sexuality, (4) one or more moral reasons common in their culture.

TALKING ABOUT SEXUAL IDENTITY AND SAME-SEX RELATIONSHIPS

Before discussing the moral issues, it is important to be as clear as possible about what people mean by commonly used terms. On a simple level, children are identified as girls or boys based on their *natal* sex. Natal sex refers to sexual identity based on visible sex organs present at birth. There are some variations: for example, some children have both a penis and a vagina. As children grow, they are treated differently by peers and adults based on their appearance as boys or girls. Most societies have different clothes and activities considered right, or at least normal, for girls and boys, women and men. The terms *boys*, *girls*, *men*, and *women* are gender terms and not sex terms. *Gender* refers to the cultural aspect of sexuality that is only remotely linked to biological sex characteristics such as genitals and

4. Gen 19:4–8 (NIV).
5. Judg 19 (NIV).
6. Lev 18:22; 20:13 (NIV).
7. For example, 1 Cor 6:9–10; 1 Tim 1:8–11 (NIV).
8. For example, Friedman and Dolansky, *The Bible Now*.
9. For example, Coogan, *What the Bible*.

hormones. The permissible similarities in clothing and activities between the genders vary from culture to culture and from historical era to era. The prohibitions on what women and men can wear come from many sources, such as law, religion, tradition, and families.

Sexuality is commonly thought of in terms of distinct categories, which works for communication purposes but does not describe the experiences of some persons. A common category is heterosexual vs. homosexual referring to a person's emotional, romantic, and sexual attraction. Heterosexual women are oriented toward men and heterosexual men are oriented toward women. Homosexuals are oriented toward people of their same gender. Homosexual men are identified as *gay*, but homosexual women sometimes identify as *gay* and sometimes as *lesbian*. Bisexuals experience sexual attraction to both men and women but may emphasize one preference more than another. Bisexuals may identify primarily as a heterosexual man or woman or as a gay man or lesbian woman.

Transgendered persons are people who are not comfortable in the gender role society has assigned to them based on their natal sex. Their identities can vary. Those who want to change their biological sex have been identified as *transsexual*. A transsexual who feels like a man but has a woman's sex characteristics may feel trapped and pursue surgery. Transgendered people may be called *transmen*, or transgender men. A *transwoman*, transgender woman, or transsexual woman identifies as a woman but has the sexual characteristics of a man. As a part of their different sense of gender, some transpersons may dress according to their gender identity rather than natal sex. An older term for these persons is *transvestite*, but *cross-dresser* is more common. Perhaps you would not be surprised to learn that some people are aware of their difference from the majority of heterosexuals but are not sure about their gender identity. Such persons have been identified as *questioning*, but others use the term *genderqueer*. The acronym *LGBTQ* refers to lesbian, gay, bisexual, transgender, and questioning or queer.

DIMENSIONS OF SEXUAL IDENTITY AND SAME-SEX RELATIONSHIPS

In chapter 3, I described a six-dimensional model of human functioning using the acronym *SCOPES*. I will use those six dimensions to discuss aspects of sexual identity important to understanding the complexity of the sexual issues Christians judge as morally right or wrong. First, a review of the six dimensions. People have a *Spiritual* (S) core, which is heavily influenced by the religious beliefs of family and friends as well as personal experience. *Cognition* (C) involves thoughts, memories, and images. *Observable* (O) behavior refers to those durable patterns of behavior that form unique personalities. Psychologists commonly recognize five personality traits or behavior patterns of openness, conscientiousness, extraversion, agreeableness, and neuroticism in addition to other traits. *Physiology* (P) is the dimension that encompasses our biological state, which includes our general health, hormones, and anything we take to alter our biological functioning such as medicine, food, and drink. *Emotions* (E) are sometimes difficult to describe, but many recognize feelings as positive and negative. Emotions are part of what it takes to motivate people to act. *Social* (S) functioning refers to influence due to social context. Any given human action can be influenced by several factors including our spirituality (S), thoughts (C), personality traits (O), general health and biological functioning (P), feelings (E), and our social context (S), which involves our location, the people present, and the time of day or year. Now let us see how the model provides a framework for understanding different aspects of sexual identity.

Christians who become aware that they are different from other men and women have a challenging *Spiritual* experience. Desires for emotional, romantic, or sexual relationships with one's own sex or discomfort with one's sexuality can be disturbing when differences are summarily dismissed as sin. Spiritual well-being is vitally important to committed Christians. And commitment involves living life according to biblical principles. Sexuality is also a major part of what it means to be a person. A great deal of life for most persons is bound up in life-long loving relationships. The Christian ideal for relationships is typically portrayed as marriage, and a common desire for couples is to have children. People who are uninterested in heterosexual relationships can feel a great deal of inner distress and tension when their sexuality seems at odds with the teaching of their faith. And many Christians increase this distress by removing LGBTQ persons from church ministry or asking them to leave a church. Some Christian parents have told LGBTQ persons they don't want them around their children. For many LGBTQ persons, openness about their gender identity and sexuality means leaving their spiritual home.

Thoughts (Cognition) can be preoccupied by a search for identity. Even when a person reaches a point of clarity that he or she is gay, lesbian, bisexual, or transgender, there are still thoughts about who to tell, how to live, and how to deal with rejection. For many Christians, the *Emotions* linked to the troubling thoughts will be decidedly negative. Anger can be felt toward God and all those who offer only condemnation and insults. The whole experience can obviously be depressing when people lose friends and family members or their worth as a human being is continually challenged. And anxiety can be expected when threats of violence and damnation in the afterlife occur. Another important emotion linked to some forms of sexuality is disgust. Many people experience a strong aversion to certain types of sexual expression.

Observable behavior can be a challenge. In a nonsupportive setting, any behavioral expression of romantic interest in a person of the same sex will be condemned. Some try to fake being straight, and some have even married people of the opposite sex and had children despite their inner sense that these actions feel unnatural.

Physiological differences may not be obvious for many who identify as gay or lesbian, but some researchers have identified differences for some sexual minorities. Scientists have found evidence for chromosomal differences, but these findings are not definitive. Others find that testosterone levels are higher in heterosexual men and lesbian women. Some researchers found that a same-sex orientation occurs more frequently among twins and siblings and is more common among family members than in the general population.[10] Studies of sexual responding reveal clear and quick biological responding to sexual stimuli that is different between straight and gay men as well as between straight and lesbian women.[11] Because of the role of culture, sexuality cannot be fully accounted for by physiological factors alone.

A person's *Social* context makes a difference in dealing with sexual maturity regardless of orientation. You can imagine how different social experiences can influence the other factors of the SCOPES model. Let me illustrate a few fictitious scenarios in a list format. Think of each person as being in a Christian home and connected to a Christian church. In each scenario, I will italicize the words referring to sources of social influence.

1. An attractive girl grows up in a loving *home* with two Evangelical *parents*. She is attracted to young *men*, and they are attracted to her. She

---

10. Balswick and Balswick, "Homosexuality," in *Authentic Sexuality*, 102–15.
11. Chivers, "A Brief Update," 407–14.

falls in love with a *man* who is also loved by her parents. They marry in a *church* and have two *children*.

2. An average-looking boy is raised in the *home* of a *fundamentalist pastor* who has remarried after the *death of his first wife, the boy's mother*. His *step-mother* has *two boys* who are older and feel called to be missionaries. As he enters the teen years, he finds that he is sexually attracted to *other boys*. Although friendly with *girls in the church*, he has no romantic interest in them. Not wanting to appear different, he goes on group dates with the *youth group*. He wonders how he will ever be able to talk with someone about his feelings. He prays that *God* will change him.

3. A girl is raised by a loving *single mother* who is quite busy with work, *two younger children*, and attempts at having a personal life. The girl has a pleasant disposition and enjoys times to visit *her friends* but she's known as a tomboy—"a bit rough around the edges." One day things go horribly wrong as an *older brother of a friend* seduces her and threatens to harm her and her siblings if she says anything. She keeps her sexual abuse a secret. As she matures she finds *men* repulsive and enjoys the comfort of *other girls*. Eventually, she connects with *another young woman* with whom she shares common interests.

4. A sharp looking young man with a slightly feminine appearance grows up with a *single mom and older sister*. He gets along equally well with both *boys and girls* who respect his acting talent. After *college* and securing a *position as a teacher*, he develops a *relationship* with a colleague. They marry and seem to get along well until he reveals a secret. He often has strong desires to dress up like a woman and go out on the town. He would really like it if his wife would join him.

In each social setting there are parents, peers, siblings, pastors, and others who can make a difference in a young person's life. The words they use and the way they demonstrate love and respect can have a profound influence on the way people think about, feel toward, and act upon their romantic and sexual desires. The social setting (e.g., home, college, work) will also be a factor in how comfortable the person feels in seeking spiritual guidance or consulting a psychotherapist.

CHRISTIANITY, MORALITY, AND SAME-SEX MARRIAGE

In this section I examine attitudes toward same-sex marriage using the six dimensions of morality derived from psychological studies as discussed in chapter 3. The purpose of this analysis is to illustrate how Christians think differently about the moral issues involved in same-sex marriage. Before beginning the analysis, I want to clarify how Christians may be viewed as belonging to two major groups when it comes to social values.

There are many ways to examine the characteristics of people who identify as Christian. Because of the size of membership in the Catholic Church, which represents more than half of all Christians, we could classify Christians as Catholic or non-Catholic.[12] Although most, if not all, Christian groups offer statements about moral issues (e.g., abortion, marriage), not everybody who identifies as a member of a church accepts the official position as a personal guide to morality. For example, artificial methods of birth control violate Catholic teaching, but surveys indicate that most U.S. Catholics use birth control.

We could also look at surveys of beliefs and classify people in terms of their core beliefs. Examples of core beliefs include "The Bible is the Word of God" and "Jesus is the Son of God." This would help us identify people who are theologically conservative, but it would not necessarily indicate their moral values.

Because we are concerned about Christian morality, it makes sense to think of Christians in terms of their beliefs about right and wrong conduct. It turns out that Christians respond to survey questions as if there were two major groups, which I will refer to as *conservative* and *progressive*. When evaluating conduct as morally right or wrong, *conservative* refers to beliefs based on a literal or near-literal interpretation of specific biblical texts. In contrast, progressive Christians (sometimes called "liberal Christians") draw upon more general biblical principles when evaluating the moral correctness of an act. I will now turn to the six moral dimensions and discuss sexual orientation and same-sex marriage.

---

12. Pew Research Center, "Global Christianity," reported more than two billion Christians in the world.

Care vs. Harm

Conservatives and progressives often refer to harm when judging an act as immoral. In many contexts, the opposite of harming someone is caring for someone. Christians can point to Jesus' formulation of the second greatest commandment, which tells us to love our neighbors as ourselves.[13] Jesus' parable of the Good Samaritan illustrates caring for a beaten man in contrast to allowing him to be stranded by a roadside without treatment.[14]

Conservatives view same-sex marriage as harming the individuals and the church. Based on the verses mentioned earlier, people who engage in same-sex relations commit acts of immorality and can expect to be harmed as a result. It was this kind of thinking that led some Christians to view the AIDs epidemic as God's punishment because at first, AIDs was commonly found among gay men. This judgment is less common since AIDs spread to heterosexual adults and children. A less literal conservative view refers to harm in a spiritual sense. This perspective leaves the specific judgment about what happens to those who violate biblical teaching up to God.

Another conservative perspective focuses on the harm done to the institution of marriage. As noted above, conservatives cite biblical texts to show that a Christian view of marriage includes one man and one woman. Any other relationship harms the Christian community and society at large because it violates God's view of an orderly society.

Progressive Christians focus on the harm done to individuals who find themselves attracted to people of their own sex. To deny LGBT persons the right to marry someone they love and to enjoy intimacy is to subject them to emotional pain for their entire life. Conservative Christians cause additional harm to LGBT persons when they refuse admission to schools (e.g., Christian colleges), restrict employment opportunities, or participation in church activities.[15] The limitations on education, employment, housing, and worship result in economic hardship, social isolation, and feeling disconnected from God. Some progressive Christians point to examples of the sexual abuse of children and vulnerable adults as the reason Paul condemned same-sex relationships in his era. These harmful activities

---

13. Mark 12:31 (NIV).

14. Luke 10:25–37 (NIV).

15. To learn about emotional distress experienced by a Christian who came out as gay, see White's personal story, *Stranger at the Gate*.

are of concern, not the loving relationships of LGBT persons who desire to marry.[16]

Fairness

In a social and moral sense, fairness usually means that we have an obligation to treat people as equals. Put another way, most people believe it is immoral to treat some people better than others when it comes to the ability to live and enjoy life. Laws and policies that permit or encourage unequal treatment of people based on their gender or skin color are considered immoral. Nations and organizations grant certain rights to people who are classified as citizens or members. Citizens can usually vote and enjoy the protections and social benefits provided by their government. Most people believe all citizens ought to be treated fairly. That is, they ought to have equal access to all the privileges and benefits available to any other citizen. Same-sex marriage is an important focus because many same-sex couples cannot obtain government and company benefits unless they are married.

In March 2014, World Vision announced they changed their policy to allow a Christian in a legal same-sex marriage to be employed. As a part of their decision, they referred to two moral dimensions: fairness in terms of equal treatment and respect for authority exemplified in the word *deferring*. Here is the quote:

> But since World Vision is a multi-denominational organization that welcomes employees from more than 50 denominations, and since a number of these denominations in recent years have sanctioned same-sex marriage for Christians, the board—in keeping with our practice of deferring to church authority in the lives of our staff, and desiring to treat all of our employees equally—chose to adjust our policy. Thus, the board has modified our Employee Standards of Conduct to allow a Christian in a legal same-sex marriage to be employed at World Vision.[17]

---

16. For alternatives to conservative perspectives, see Campolo, "Homosexuality," 206–10.

17. See letter linked by Sarah Pulliam Bailey, "World Vision to Recognize," *Washington Post*, Religion News Service, March 25, 2014, https://www.washingtonpost.com/national/religion/world-vision-to-recognize-employees-same-sex-marriages/2014/03/25/a377ff8e-b42b-11e3-bab2-b9602293021d_story.html (accessed June 27, 2016)

Conservative Christian church and organization leaders responded with strong criticism to the marriage policy change and advocated that Christians ought to switch their support to other charities. The focus of the outrage was the perception that World Vision had abandoned the belief that marriage is between one man and one woman. In a quick about-face, World Vision reversed their decision after two days.[18] Although conservative Christian leaders have not argued in favor of discrimination or unequal treatment of LGBT persons, the policies of Christian schools, organizations, and churches result in unfair treatment when fairness is defined as equal treatment. Put another way, LGBT persons in romantic same-sex relationships or marriages cannot be students at Christian schools or employed at conservative Christian organizations. If they are students or employees, they need to remain celibate.[19] In addition, Christian leaders have been advocates of laws that prohibit same-sex marriage. Various stories also appear in the news of Christians refusing to treat or provide services to LGBT persons.[20]

Progressives focus on the unequal treatment of LGBT persons. They view all people as God's children and emphasize the limited role of choice when it comes to sexuality. Attempts to change sexual orientation based on prayer and psychotherapy have rarely been successful but often cause harm. Demanding that people change their sexuality or live a celibate life to enjoy the benefits of heterosexuals places an unfair burden on LGBT persons whether in a Christian community or society. Progressives do not find evidence in the Bible that the texts about sexual activity between people of the same sex were about people in loving relationships. In addition, the biblical reference to Adam and Eve does not logically preclude other marriage relationships. After all, God did not condemn polygamy, which presumably he would have condemned if marriage was to be restricted to one man and one woman in order to enjoy God's blessings.

Loyalty vs. Betrayal

In the Bible, God warns people against unfaithfulness. People who leave God's way to follow the ways of other gods are likened to people who commit adultery. Couples expect each other to be faithful. Having intimate

---

18. Gracy and Weber, "World Vision Reverses."
19. Stern, "Christian College to LGBTQ Students."
20. Phillip, "Pediatrician Refuses"; Blair, "Christian Bakers."

relationships with others is counted as a serious betrayal of the relationship. Similarly, organizations and nations demand members and citizens to be loyal. At a national level, some acts of betrayal count as treason.

Conservative Christians expect people to be loyal to the family of God, which includes following rules and not engaging in protests against church teaching or flagrantly acting against God's ways. Sex outside of a marriage between a man and a woman is the two-thousand-year-old tradition of the church based on a pervasive interpretation of biblical texts. The recent re-interpretations of the biblical text to affirm same-sex relationships, including marriage, violate the way God has guided the church for centuries. People advocating for same-sex marriage are betrayers of the faith.

Progressive Christians argue that LGBT persons maintain their loyalty to God and to biblical teaching as they interpret it. They point to obvious examples (e.g., Lutherans, Presbyterians, Baptists) of church groups and individual congregations who were disloyal to a parent church when they broke fellowship to establish a new church group based upon a different interpretation of a biblical text. Progressive Christians also point out the failure of church organizations to quickly and publicly denounce slavery, clergy sexual abuse of children, and the oppression of women as examples that justify challenging church leadership. Such challenges can indeed appear like betrayal, but they are in fact moral because they represent loyalty to God's perspective of love and respect for all persons. And the challenges represent loyalty to Jesus' criticism of the way religious leaders interpreted the laws of Moses in his day.[21] Moreover, challenges to traditional teaching reflects a loyalty to the practical way the early church leaders debated which rules new Christians ought to follow.[22]

Authority and Respect

All groups of people expect people within their group to show respect for the group's leaders and policies. This expectation of respect for authority is true of businesses, schools, and governments as well as churches. Conservative Christians easily point to biblical texts to show that God demands respect. God is the ultimate authority, and the Bible reveals God's expectations for personal conduct. To violate God's commands is to show disrespect for God in addition to disrespect for the people God has entrusted

---

21. See Matt 23:1–4 (NIV).
22. See Acts 15:1–41 (NIV).

to be leaders. As creator, God created only two sexes and declared rules for how they should and should not have sexual relations. Even when people see no harm in breaking one of God's rules, they ought to follow God's rules because God knows what is best for them and for all of humanity.

Progressive Christians recognize the importance of respect for God, the Bible, and leaders in society and the church. Progressive Christians argue that they simply disagree with the way conservative groups have interpreted the Bible. They also find that the way conservatives view sexual minorities represents a disrespectful attitude based on the arrogant belief that the religious leaders are the only ones in a position to know how God's rules should be interpreted. Progressive Christians point to examples of church reformers that spoke out against religious authorities throughout history. And as noted above, Jesus himself spoke out against the way Jewish authorities of his day interpreted the laws of Moses.

Purity and Sanctity vs. Degradation

Conservative Christians do not follow the Hebrew ceremonial laws governing washing and identifying some animals as clean and others as unclean. But they are mindful that God's character is reflected in these ancient laws. Following Jesus' teaching, Christians are concerned to maintain a pure heart and a holy life. The cleansing of the inner person comes through repentance of sin. As we have seen, biblical texts identify same-sex relations as sinful; thus; both the sex act and the accompanying same-sex relationships and marriage are not compatible with a pure and holy life.

Progressive Christians believe LGBT persons can have a relationship with God. When God indwells them through his spirit, they are redeemed as whole persons. As redeemed people, they are pure and holy unto God. As noted before, progressive Christians view the oft cited biblical texts as representing a perverted and disrespectful form of sexuality bearing no resemblance to people in loving same-sex relationships who desire to marry.

Liberty vs. Oppression

The Exodus story is the quintessential example of liberation from oppression. Although Christians do not celebrate the Passover as Jews do, they do recognize God's liberating power and the importance of resisting oppression. Conservative Christians encourage people to be free from the burden of sin, which includes forbidden sexual activity and relationships that are different from God's original plan. To live a life that is contrary to God's rules is to live a life in bondage, which will ultimately lead to eternal punishment.

Progressive Christians focus on liberating LGBT persons from the oppression of religious and social rules that keep them from enjoying a fulfilled life in a loving relationship with another person. They not only point to Jesus' teaching about loving others, but they also point to Jesus' teaching about a new way of living that is free from the old laws. For example, Jesus taught that people could not put new wine in old wine bottles, suggesting that he was offering a new way of life. Also, as noted above, progressives point to the attempt of the early church leaders to reduce the unnecessary burden of old rules, which new Christians were required to keep.[23] Today, Christian leaders are advised to consider which old rules should be kept and which ones should be let go in order to promote freedom in Christ rather than keep people chained to old ways of thinking.

CONCLUSION

Both conservative and progressive Christians may make additional arguments about how to interpret the applicable biblical texts and how to view the issues involved in treating sexual minorities and the desire of some for same-sex marriage. I do not presume to address all the issues or enter into detailed analyses of the biblical texts. For many Christians, the key decision will turn on what the Bible says. And that, of course, is the focus of much dissension.

Some Christians agree that the biblical texts clearly refer to same-sex sexual activity as prohibited behavior but disagree on what biblical rules apply to contemporary Christians and what rules only apply to those in Israelite culture or the culture of the early church.

Christians who believe that homosexual relationships are sinful and that same-sex marriage in particular is also a sinful departure from God's plan are quick to point out that God calls Christians to treat people with love and respect. They also observe that all people are sinners and in need of redemption. Some feel that one sin is not worse than another. Considering these perspectives, the church ought to be supportive of people attempting

---

23. See the debate over rules for Gentiles and Jews in Acts 15.

to understand their sexuality. A loving and caring attitude offers lifelong support through fellowship and encouragement.

Finally, some advocate maintaining relationships with LGBT persons and trusting that God's spirit will do the work of convicting people of any sin in their lives when people seek to live in a right relationship with God.

SUMMARY

In this chapter, I presented information about sexual identity to help us think about the relevant factors to consider when deciding if same-sex marriage is morally right or wrong. First I reviewed the range of terms used to refer to people who have different sexual identities than that of the heterosexual majority. In addition to people attracted to members of their own sex, some are attracted to people of both sexes. Moreover, some people do not identify as having the same gender, as might be suggested by their biological sex characteristics.

In the second part of the chapter, I viewed various aspects of sexual identity by reference to the six dimensions (i.e., SCOPES) of functioning described in chapter 3. The intent of this presentation was to remind us that the moral issues of concern are not just about a biological sex act or an act of marriage but involve a person's spiritual identity (S), thoughts (C), established behavior patterns (O), physiological characteristics (P), feelings or emotions (E), and social (S) influences.

In the final section, I considered several moral perspectives Christians offer when discussing same-sex relationships or marriage. I observed that people are often divided into two major groups of conservatives and progressives when it comes to views about moral values. An important focus for Christians is how to interpret a set of key biblical texts related to same-sex activity and marriage. In working through the analysis, I referred to six dimensions derived from moral psychology research to show how Christians may arrive at different appraisals of moral conduct. These appraisals often focus on one or more of the six dimensions: harm, fairness, loyalty, respect for authority, purity, and oppression.

I leave you with a final statement as a guide in thinking about Christian morality and same-sex marriage: Christian moral judgment about same-sex marriage is based on an interpretation of biblical texts, an understanding of human nature, an understanding of human sexuality, and one or more moral reasons influenced by culture.

ADDITIONAL RESOURCES

1. See the article by Elizabeth Dias, "A Change of Heart: Inside the Evangelical War over Gay Marriage" in *Time*, January 26, 2015. You can find it at time.com or your library.

2. Search www.ChristianityToday.com for recent news articles related to LGBT and same-sex marriage issues.

3. Search www.Barna.org for recent surveys revealing attitudes of Christians and non-Christians toward LGBT and same-sex marriage issues.

4. See the *Theology of Sex* booklet available from the National Association of Evangelicals at www.NAE.net.

5. Search online to learn the official position about homosexuality and same-sex marriage published by your church or a religious group that interests you.

6. Read the June 26, 2015, text from the U.S. Supreme Court, which included an analysis of human rights as part of their decision that same-sex couples have the right to marry in the United States. http://www.supremecourt.gov/opinions/14pdf/14-556_3204.pdf.

DISCUSSION QUESTIONS

1. Read or listen to a statement about same-sex marriage or LGBT rights by Christian leaders. Which of the six moral dimensions can you identify? What is the order in which the dimensions appear? For example, did they begin talking about harm first, or did they begin by referring to the authority of God's word or another of the six dimensions?

2. How closely do you agree with the position of your church or organization? If you hold different views, why do you hold those views?

3. Some Christians say, "love the sinner, hate the sin" to illustrate their approach to caring about LGBT persons but rejecting their sexual activity and same-sex marriages as sinful. What do you think about this phrase?

4. What does it mean for Christians to love their neighbors as themselves? This is a follow-up to the previous question and requires an answer to the question, "What is Christian love?"

REFERENCES

Allman, Jaimée. "Resilience and Forgiveness in a Lesbian Sample: An Exploratory Study." MS thesis, Evangel University, 2009.

Balswick, Judith K., and Jack O. Balswick. *Authentic Human Sexuality: An Integrated Approach*. 2nd ed. Downers Grove: IVP, 2008.

Blair, Leonardo. "Christian Bakers Who Refused to Make Cake for Lesbian Wedding Found Guilty of Discrimination; Will Have to Pay Up to $150K." *Christian Post*, February 4, 2015, http://www.christianpost.com/news/christian-bakers-who-refused-to-make-cake-for-lesbian-wedding-found-guilty-of-discrimination-will-have-to-pay-up-to-150k-133581/ (accessed June 27, 2016).

Campolo, Tony. "Homosexuality." In *Adventures in Missing the Point: How the Culture-Controlled Church Neutered the Gospel*, edited by Brian D. McLaren and Tony Campolo, 198–215. Grand Rapids: Zondervan, 2003.

Chivers, Meredith. "A Brief Update on the Specificity of Sexual Arousal." *Sexual and Relationship Therapy* 25 (2010) 407–14.

Coogan, Michael. *What the Bible Really Says about Sex*. New York: Twelve, 2010.

Dias, Elizabeth. "A Change of Heart: Inside the Evangelical War over Gay Marriage." *Time*, January 26, 2015, 44–48.

Friedman, Richard E., and Shawna Dolansky. *The Bible Now*. New York: Oxford University Press, 2012.

Gracey, Celeste, and Jeremy Weber. "World Vision Reverses Decision to Hire Christians in Same-Sex Marriages." *Christianity Today*, March 26, 2014, http://www.christianitytoday.com/ct/2014/march-web-only/world-vision-reverses-decision-gay-same-sex-marriage.html (accessed June 27, 2016).

National Association of Evangelicals. *Theology of Sex: Restoring God's Intentions for Sex*. National Association of Evangelicals, 2012, http://nae.net/theology-of-sex/ (accessed June 27, 2016).

Pew Research Center. "Global Christianity—A Report on the Size and Distribution of the World's Christian Population." PewForum, December 19, 2011, http://www.pewforum.org/2011/12/19/global-christianity-exec/ (accessed June 27, 2016)

Phillip, Abby. "Pediatrician Refuses to Treat Baby with Lesbian Parents and There's Nothing Illegal about It." *Washington Post*, February 19, 2015, http://www.washingtonpost.com/news/morning-mix/wp/2015/02/19/pediatrician-refuses-to-treat-baby-with-lesbian-parents-and-theres-nothing-illegal-about-it/ (accessed June 27, 2016).

Stern, Mark Joseph. "Christian Colleges to LGBTQ Students: You're Not Welcome Here." *Slate*, July 16, 2014. http://www.slate.com/blogs/outward/2014/07/16/christian_colleges_discriminate_against_gay_and_trans_students_and_faculty.html.

White, Mel. *Stranger at the Gate: To Be Gay and Christian in America*. New York: Plume, 1995.

9

A Woman's Place: Perspectives on Gender Equality

Ruth V. Burgess

The overbearing equator sun knew no difference between the dark brown parched earth and the varied hues of brown bodies that stood at attention on the granite steps of the 113-year-old mission bungalow during April 1947. They were waiting for the new superintendent and his family from the United States to arrive from Poona.

Recently, Miss Jessie Ferguson, known as Maoushi Bai, had managed the Junnar Boys Orphanage for over a decade. Being ill she turned the responsibilities over to Reverend Theodore Vassar and the Assemblies of God denomination.

Social unrest was rampant as Mother India strove to rid herself and children from centuries-old British colonialism. Thousands had been killed during these freedom attempts. In addition, the Mohammedans (Muslims) were fighting to separate from Hindustan and form their country to be known as Pakistan. Trains belching coal ash held the bodies of murdered passengers when they arrived at both border entry points weekly.

The first time I met the frail Jugtap girl, who sported a wide smile with sparkling white teeth but kept her black eyes focused on the ground, was when Miss Ferguson gave the fourteen year old to my mother, Estelle Vassar. The spinster said my mother would be too busy with seventy-eight orphans to care for and needed an ayah (nurse maid) to help nurture my eighteen-month sister. From the way the teenager draped her saffron and black colored sari between the legs meant she was a Hindu. ("Uhm, maybe she could become our first convert to Christianity?")

No one could remember if the Jugtap girl had a first name. She had never been to school. But it did not really matter because her father was dead. Maoushi Bai permitted the Jugtap girl's mother to sweep the debris from around the mission compound for a penance. The young teenager had been engaged to an "old man" at the age of three years. Now, Estelle would not have a nameless person around. After consultations, our new ayah and friend took the name of Lillie Bai Jugtap and, being somewhat capricious, I playfully began pulling the extra sari cloth down from her backside so she would look like a Christian girl while in the mission bungalow.

After two years Lillie Bai took water baptism, which meant the Government of India recognized her as a Christian. But her uncle Sumboo was concerned that the "old man" would come and claim Lillie Bai as his wife. Knowing his age and possible immanent death, the aged groom could claim the young teenager, since she was promised to him at the age of three years. At this time in the villages, suttee was practiced. The widows were burned alive on the flaming biers of their husband's corpse. Their religion believed that in an earlier reincarnation a wife had caused the death of her husband, who was considered her Lord. Then Sumboo raised the question, "Might the aged groom accept a payoff for the now Christian wife—his child bride?"

After five and a half years, Lillie Bai Jugtap married Vasant Saraf in a Christian ceremony with a wedding feast. Their home was blessed with two sons when she became pregnant with their third child. Lillie Bai was cleaning her mud hut when some dirt covered with cow manure was seen shifting in the corner. Getting a stone and starting to shove it in the hole a king cobra's head surfaced and bit Lillie Bai on her finger. Quickly she called Vasant and friends saying someone must kill the cobra and she needed to go to the dispensary.

With family members she walked to the dispensary. The attendant said, "Your bite is from a rat, not from a sap. Go home and put some Dettol on it." They walked back to the hut.

Lillie Bai began to have a piercing headache and her body ached. The pregnant mother said, "It was a sap. Take me back to the dispensary." They walked slowly back the second time to the dispensary. Her baby lay still in the amniotic fluid. The attendant said, "Why are you here? You have a rat bite. Go home and drink some cool water." They walked painfully and slowly back to the hut.

Soon her body began to swell, her eyes turned red, and she could hardly breathe. Lillie Bai pled with her family to help her. Lillie Bai died that afternoon of a king cobra's bite. When her family went to

CHRISTIAN MORALITY—PART TWO

the dispensary, the attendant said, "Why are you here? She was but a woman."

—But a Woman, Lillie Bai Jugtap Saraf[1]

INTRODUCTION AND OVERVIEW

THE PURPOSE OF THIS chapter is to assert that gender inequalities constitute a global human rights problem. These inequities are evident when we examine prejudice, discrimination, war, violence, distorted interpretations of religious texts, physical and mental abuse, poverty, and disease. These inequities tend to fall disproportionately on women and girls. From a moral perspective, Christians, who believe that they were created in the image of the triune God, should work toward fair and equal treatment for women and men. This theological premise requires that people take moral action when injustices occur. When people intervene, they become part of the solution. Both genders have equal worth in creation and life. Thus, they have equal responsibility to advocate for equal rights for women. In this sense, both men and women may be considered feminists.

Feminism has become a loaded term in contemporary society. For the purposes of this chapter, we will understand feminism to be, essentially, a human rights movement seeking to remove implicit and explicit restrictions against women and advocating for the advancement and emancipation of women and girls in all aspects of society: religious, political, and socioeconomic. Because of a long history of discrimination, women have suffered ignominy in most cultures.[2]

In this chapter, popular western religious-political terms such as *conservative*, *progressive*, or *liberal*, will not be used. Labels tend to be polarizing rather than being productive in problem solving.

As an alternative to labeling, Reuven Feuerstein suggests there are three basic influences on our thinking.[3] Our first and basic impressions are those learned through the transmission of heritage and tradition. Next are the personal experiences we encounter. These societal practices may

---

1. Editor's note: The story of Lillie Bai is by the chapter author, Ruth Burgess.

2. Concern has been expressed over the use of the word "feminism" and a preference to use the word "womanism." Sequences of phonemes are not innately bad. Rather, it is the semantic meanings people attach that affect the popularity of "phonemic use."

3. Feuerstein et al., "The Dynamic," 131–36.

be complementary with one's tradition, or they may be divergent. The predominant or power culture may view other cultures as subcultures (lower in esteem and given limited access to resources) or co-cultures. These complementary practices are viewed positively, and intercultural transmission of values and resources may be encouraged.

Scientific learning, the third basic influence, provides an orderly system to further one's knowledge, use knowledge skills, acquire literacy systems, and support reasonable habits of the mind and spirit. The rise of scientific thought and its methods continues to influence both tradition and experience.

Learning Outcomes

After reading this chapter and collaborating with others, the reader will be able to:

1. Propose a plan to bring social justice via the emancipation of women in religious, political, and socioeconomic venues.
2. Contrast civil and religious systemic approaches toward altering gender inequality.
3. Use a reasoned, Christian, and moral perspective while participating in a systematic, guided, and mediated learning experience critiquing inequities used against women.

Organization

Five sections comprise the remaining parts of this chapter. In Section I, you will read brief sections of the United Nations Charter. The *Universal Declaration of Human Rights* document prescribes that committed members promote "universal respect for, and observance of human rights and fundamental freedoms for all without distinction as to race, sex, language, or religion." Section II, "A Moral Dilemma in a Secular Setting," illustrates early perspectives relating to obtaining gender equity. In this secular case study, a group of female university professors contested discriminatory practices. Section III, "Insights Found in Early Stories Thought Religious," introduces gender discriminatory beliefs among the disciples. In Section IV, "Step Forward and Engage in Dialogue for Gender Equity," you are encouraged to engage in a form of reasoned advocacy by using either of the narratives: *But a Woman*, by Ruth Burgess, or *Lament of the Daughters*, by Carol Wiseman. An exercise guides you systematically through five thoughtful action steps: Awareness, Metalog and Metacognition, Inquiry, Reflection, Advocacy, and Presentation. Section V contains the chapter summary.

A First Exercise

Let us begin our inquiry into morality and gender by thinking about the opening account of Lillie Bai. As you read, identify the moral injustice issues in the first narrative. Ask yourself, "Through what lenses am I formulating my thoughts?" For instance, are they from a Western or Eastern cultural vantage point? Did you arrive at these issues from your heritage, personal experiences, or scientific thinking?

SECTION I: THE UNIVERSAL DECLARATION OF HUMAN RIGHTS

In this first section, you will read an excerpt from the Universal Declaration of Human Rights, which was ratified in 1948. This text provides a basis for considering the dignity and worth of all people (italics added for emphasis).

> PREAMBLE. Whereas recognition of the inherent dignity and of the equal and inalienable *rights of all members of the human family* is the foundation of freedom, justice and peace in the world . . .
>
> Whereas the peoples of the United Nations have in the Charter reaffirmed their faith in fundamental human rights, in the dignity and worth of the human person *and in the equal rights of men and women* and have determined to promote social progress and better standards of life in larger freedom.
>
> Article 1. *All human beings* are born free and equal in dignity and rights.
>
> Article 2. Everyone is entitled to all the rights and freedoms set forth in this Declaration, *without distinction of any kind*, such as race, color, sex, language, religion, political or other opinion, national or social origin, property, birth or other status.
>
> Article 5. No one shall be subjected to torture or to cruel, inhuman or degrading treatment or punishment.

Article 16. (1) Men and women *of full age*, without any limitation due to race, nationality or religion, have the right to marry and to found a family. They are entitled *to equal rights as to marriage, during marriage and at its dissolution.*

Article 23. (2) Everyone, without any discrimination, *has the right to equal pay for equal work.*

Article 25. (2) *Motherhood and childhood are entitled to special care and assistance.* All children, whether born in or out of wedlock, shall enjoy the same social protection.[4]

SECTION II: A MORAL DILEMMA IN A SECULAR SETTING

Equity in gender matters usually does not exist or continue unless it is monitored. Like the political system known as democracy, gender equity requires people to be active participants.

A Brief History of Gender Discrimination

In the last half of the twentieth century, feminists began to be more adamant that women were not being included equitably in all aspects of society. Sure, the suffragettes had marched and received voting rights for women in the early twentieth century. But besides casting ballots, few women were encouraged to attain positions of power or leadership. There was a gender pay gap (i.e., women received less pay than did men). Despite their accomplishments and performance, employers would usually employ and promote men more quickly than women. The term *glass ceiling* meant that society kept women from achieving positions of greater perceived value—they could look at the male patriarchy or the "good old boys" above them but would not be able to attain such positions.

In addition to equal pay, feminists advocated for equal opportunities in receiving scholarships, hiring practices, and equal rights. This called for legal action. From this advocacy emerged *Title IX*, the federal civil rights law that prohibits sex discrimination in education. Results of the implementation of *Title IX* are particularly recognizable in women's sports.

---

4. The full text can be found on the Internet. "The Universal Declaration of Human Rights," United Nations, accessed June 17, 2016, www.un.org/en/documents/charter/.

Current Gender Issues

As we look to the twenty-first-century, statistics show continued safety issues for women attending institutions of education. A campus study found that 28 percent of women, while in institutions of higher education, will be victims of sexual assault and attempted sexual assault.[5]

Moreover, implicit harassment at work continues to occur, yet 62 percent of women who report harassment take no action.[6] It seems women have an intense fear of incrimination, both explicitly and implicitly. But why? Have stereotypes stunted the attainment of fair and just systems with protections for both genders? What system exists that can be accessed to address injustices and bring just resolutions?

An Example: How University Women Addressed Inequality

One such politically sensitive narrative took place in the early 1990s deep in the Bible belt of the U.S. Southwest Missouri State University (i.e., SMSU, now Missouri State University) is located in the Ozark Mountains. Historically, this area of the state had been slower to develop economically and, some would say, politically.

SMSU had not openly addressed women's rights equitably on its two campuses. The freedoms and entitlements of women had been largely ignored or suppressed by local custom and behavior. Women of SMSU were not calling for equality because they differentiated local university practices from general human rights issues.

After observing or experiencing either gender discrimination or harassment, seven full-time women professors who were tenured from varied departments across campus met for two years in secret to plan a fair and legally supported course of action. We thought we were *safer* than were younger professors. In other words they were more *vulnerable* and might experience some form of harassment or discrimination if they knew or participated in the new evolving organization. We called the group Women's Issues Network (WIN).

---

5. American Association of University Women, "AAUW Issues," para. 1.
6. George Washington University, "Sexual Harassment," para. 4.

Defining the Mission

In 1992, the following WIN Mission Statement was accepted: "To provide faculty women with the information and support necessary for success in their jobs and their lives; serve as an advocacy group for equal opportunity and equal treatment of women in matters of appointments, professional support, tenure, and promotions; and provide a forum for campus issues important to women."[7]

Collecting Evidence

After gathering campus-wide incidences of discrimination and harassment, a tentative plan was developed. The group conferred with representatives of the Title IX Office in Kansas City. Two research studies were underway. The first was to secure interest from other faculty women. Many of those respondents expressed fear that they might lose their jobs if they participated. Others were curious—were we going to be a *radical* group or a *sane* group? Even some of the older, full professors replied that they were behind us but could not be seen with the WIN group for fear of further retribution. Fear and intimidation were the main concerns. By now WIN was becoming an open enrollment group. On January 28, 1993, there were fifteen female professors who were perceived as a caucus group.

The other project was a matched-pairs study. We measured the number of years it took matched female and male faculty to move from being hired on a tenure track to becoming an instructor, assistant professor, associate professor, and full professor. During the process, we also gathered data about how many men and women were at each level over a five-year period. The number of men increased over the number of women significantly as tenure and promotions occurred.

Seeking Action

After gathering data, we looked forward to meeting with the acting president of the university. We wanted action from both the administration and board of governors. Earlier, our predecessors had attempted to work through departmental and college committees but were unsuccessful. This

---

7. The statements and related quotations are from the author's notes.

CHRISTIAN MORALITY—PART TWO

time we had reviewed the law, research, and case studies. The following goals were presented to the higher administration:

1. Employ a university-wide affirmative action officer and provide a staff for this office. (There was no office or officer charged with insuring equal opportunity and equal treatment for women.) The findings of this officer shall be open to the public.
2. Establish a "Women's Center."
3. Advocate for global gender equity policies.
4. Address and stop gender harassment and discrimination.
5. Prevent campus bullying and violence.
6. Begin diversity and gender equity training for all levels (e.g., administration, faculty, staff, students, news media).
7. Clarify fair ethics that apply in the campus workplace.
8. Post legal issues in management and hiring.
9. Specify clear and open records relating to promotions and tenure.
10. Document clear and open appeal policies and procedures.
11. Implement assistance plans to develop skills that support equal opportunities.
12. Create a Gender Studies program.
13. Develop an SMSU long-range plan for insuring equal opportunities.
14. Provide a yearly status report on salaries, ranks, professional development support, and experience categorized according to gender.
15. Conduct a curriculum review as to where gender issues are learned in the General Education program.
16. Distribute a written committee report relating to the promotion of women to all levels of administration and faculty-ranked level.
17. Submit a written statement supporting the appointment of women and minorities to the Board of Regents by the governor of Missouri.

Outcomes

Within a year, a permanent university president whose primary focus was athletics was selected. Soon, female staff asked to join WIN. Student organizations also wished to be included. After polling the active membership, it was decided to open WIN to the staff and, at a later date, to consider inviting students.

Although progress was made, at the beginning of the twenty-first century financial discrepancies persisted between genders within university departments. In order to bring about reasoned and reasonable advancement, fair-minded individuals need to be vigilant. In a nation where there is a division between church and state, civil laws provide a means to engage in participatory democracy if we but use them.

SECTION III: MORAL TEMPLATES FOUND IN EARLY STORIES THOUGHT RELIGIOUS

When one considers religious sensitivities, what resolutions are available when discriminatory acts are perpetrated against women? Examples of maledictions can be seen when pundits accept only portions of stories or scriptures, ignore feminine attributes of the Triune Creator God, diminish the wisdom and acts of valor conducted by women, demand servitude, falsely diminish a woman's character, and even falsely accuse women if it will benefit the male image or power system. These practices are examples of moral malfunctions.

Established religions share a beginning, the development of policies, laws, and procedures, and maintain procreative systems. During this process, moral codes are developed. But the question emerges: Who were the leaders and scribes that determined what was to become holy writ? These culture-bearers were educated or esteemed men.

Interestingly, there are biblical images of God portraying feminine as well as male characteristics. These feminine characteristics are frequently ignored in pulpit sermons. Some of these images are a woman in the process of giving birth, God as a nursing mother, God as midwife, God as baker, God as dame wisdom, God as mother bear, God as mother eagle, and God as mother hen. In addition, the religious male hierarchy continued to propagate the myth that blamed women for the fall of man and implied they are lesser creations and should live with pain and guilt-burdened lives.

The past three hundred years have opened up new possibilities for the stories found in world religions. As scholars studied different translations and additional scrolls were found—or alternate manuscripts were made available—scholars discovered that women had been purposefully omitted from stories. Destruction of heretical manuscripts had been encouraged. Books by women during the years that the other four Gospels were written had been omitted. There are cases where masculinizing of feminine names in the New Testament was accepted. Mary Magdalene was scandalized for centuries by the male religious hierarchy as a harlot when in old texts she was reported to be a beloved leader of first-century Christianity.

The Rock of the Church Blasts Women

Let us take a step back into the first century CE and read a conversation among Jesus' leadership group following his crucifixion. The Galileans appear rattled and want to know what secrets Jesus shared with Mary and not with them. Their negative attitude toward women, in this case, Mary Magdalene, is apparent when they discount what Jesus would share with a woman.

The scholars of the *Jesus Seminar* collaborated to collect and translate noncanonical gospels and fragments in *The Complete Gospels: Annotated Scholars Version*.[8] Of particular interest in this chapter are portions of the *Gospel of Thomas* and the *Gospel of Mary*. In the *Gospel of Thomas*, we read that Simon Peter wants Jesus to banish Mary from the leadership group:

> Simon Peter said to them, "Make Mary leave us, for females don't deserve life." Jesus said, "Look, I will guide her to make her male, so that she too may become a living spirit resembling you males. For every female who makes herself male will enter the domain of Heaven."[9]

According to Miller, the transition of female to male is used as a metaphor for translation from earthly to heavenly existence, from mortality to immortality. Perhaps this was a pragmatic approach since female philosophers often disguised themselves as men.[10] Another interpretation could be that Jesus would teach women how to think abstractly and critically and not

---

8. Noncanonical writings are documents that are not a part of the Bible.
9. Miller, *The Complete Gospels*, 322.
10. Ibid., 322.

remain in sensorial cultural conditions. Until centuries later, only women from prestigious families had an option for a secular education. Certainly this was not a physical transformation, but one relating to mind and spirit.

The *Gospel of Mary* is thought to have been written late in the first century or early second century. This piece represents the different options among the apostles. Interestingly, this is the time period when the commonly accepted four canonical gospels were written.

> Jesus continued, "This is why you get sick and die, for you love what deceives you. Anyone with a mind should use it to think!"
>
> Then Mary stood up. She greeted them all and addressed her brothers. "Do not weep and be distressed nor let your hearts be irresolute. For his grace will be with you all and will shelter you. Rather we should praise his greatness, for he has joined us together and made us true human beings." When Mary said these things, she turned their minds toward the Good, and they began to ask about the words of the Savior.[11]

Peter then asks Mary to teach and share personal conversation with the Savior. The teaching refers to mind, body, and spirit. (Four manuscript pages are missing.)

> Peter said to Mary, "Sister, we know that the Savior loved you more than any other woman. Tell us the words of the Savior that you know, but which we haven't heard." Mary responded, "I will report to you as much as I remember that you don't know."
>
> Andrew said, "Brothers, what is your opinion of what was just said? I for one don't believe that the Savior said these things because these opinions seem to be so different from his thought."
>
> After reflecting on these matters, Peter said, "Has the Savior spoken secretly to a woman and not openly so that we would all hear? Surely he did not wish to indicate that she is more worthy than are we?"
>
> Then Mary wept and said to Peter, "Peter, my brother, what are you imagining about this? Do you think that I've made all this up secretly by myself or that I am telling lies about the Savior?"
>
> Levi said to Peter, "Peter, you have a constant inclination to anger and you are always ready to give way to it. And even now you are doing exactly that by questioning the woman as if you're her adversary. If the Savior considered her to be worthy, who are

---

11. Ibid., 361–62.

you to disregard her? For he knew her completely and loved her devotedly."[12]

Mothers and Grannies of Twentieth-Century Pentecost

While society ignored the remnant of early church feminism for centuries, Swan reminds us of spiritual acts recorded by the desert Mothers.[13] These women exhibited compassion, used prophetic freedom, shared the gift of life, and demonstrated leadership as they built monasteries in the desert. Many righteous women became martyrs in this new religion now titled *Christianity*.

Subsequently, new Christian groups have evolved throughout the centuries. In the early twentieth century, a prophetic group known as "the Pentecostals" emerged. They emphasized a spirit-filled life and the soon coming of Jesus Christ to take his bride away. Similar to the first-century Christian Church, and before the organizational formation of structure and power, Pentecostals broke with many traditional practices. They were "spirit-formed, spirit-led, and spirited." Hence, both women and men could be called into this end-of-time ministry.

Women of Pentecost displayed the Gifts of the Spirit by being prophetesses, evangelists, pastors, teachers, and serving as beloved mothers and grannies of these new churches. In addition, these women-of-the-calling founded churches, Bible schools, denominations, orphanages, and communes. They prayed for the sick and waited in prayer for souls to be saved and redeemed. Frequently, women reported hearing the voice of God calling them to be missionaries in foreign lands. In the United States these spirited women were feeling a sense of spiritual liberation.

Does history repeat itself? Frequently, change is supplanted with the generational continuity of suppression of women in Christian ministry. By the second and third generations in the new Pentecostal movement, when the "It's-the-male-God's-will" approach was adopted by the power structure, women found themselves excluded or their voices minimized. However, once Pentecostal traditions had advocated for the priesthood of all believers they maintained selected elevated positions that were filled by men. Hence, practice and polity differed from early Pentecostal scriptural

12. Ibid., 363–65.
13. Swan, *The Forgotten*.

interpretation. The restoring of founding beliefs and outward practices requires action. One of these is righting the wrongs perpetuated against women in ministry at all levels.

SECTION IV: ENGAGE IN DIALOGUE FOR GENDER EQUITY

In the *Lament of the Daughters*, poet Carol Wiseman addresses the status of women within the church hierarchy,[14] relating particularly to some Evangelical and Pentecostal denominations. Wiseman differentiates between men being the oppressors of God's daughters when in reality it is God's battle between the seed of Eve and the enemy of God—Satan.

"Lament of the Daughters" (Excerpt)

How long O God, how long?
How long must we travail without a covering?
How long will you leave us in bondage
    in oppression?
Would we have been better off in Egypt?
How long will our cries for freedom
Be ignored, be silenced,
How long will they fall on deaf ears?
On defiant platforms?

How long O God will our voices be silent,
Our hands desolate to perform thy great works,
Our gifts be unopened, our healing hands prevented
Our prophetic words refused?
How long before the war has overcome our brothers
Who refuse to allow us to help heal?
How long Oh God of Eve, of Rachael, of Mary
Before this day's daughters might

---

14. Carol is a biblical feminist scholar and founder and director of the Center for Faith Leadership.

> Perform the miracles you placed within them?
> Will you circumcise again?
> Will you circumcise the hearts of men?
> that the daughters today might birth
> the gifts within them, as Sarah and Mary
> birthed the miracle you placed within them?
> The travail is so long, so hard, so painful.
> It is not for ourselves we cry out, but for those
> Oh God who keep us in bondage
> For it is their freedom that we seek,
>
> How long must Rachael weep?
> How long must we travail with divine gifts
> > pent up inside us?
> How long will bondage remain?
> Let this day be the end, Oh Mighty Creator of All
> Let the hearts of the Fathers turn toward you
> With right understanding that your daughters
> > were created at your hand; equal
> Created as your partners and theirs.
> How Long?[15]

In secular systems there are civil laws and policies that may provide guidance and security when addressing gender inequities. In religious circles, there may be an absence of policies or discussions about gender equality. If policies are present, they often lack enforcement. When feminists attempt to hold discussions, they may be subjected to intimidation. For example, some may say the person is "not acting like a Christian" if alternate perspectives are given. These "gatekeepers" of an antiquated system reach towards a mystical domain that supports male domination over women.

How can fair-minded people enter into cross-cultural, moral-based dialogues? One approach may be through mediated learning dialogues.

---

15. Wiseman, "Lament," 201.

This approach is organized in a manner that allows different information to be integrated in a mediated process, which you will find in the next section.

SECTION V: STEP FORWARD: A CRITICAL REASONING EXERCISE

This final section of the chapter provides an opportunity for readers to collaborate with others in a mediated learning exercise. First, select "Lament of the Daughters" or "But a Woman" by Lillie Bai Jugtap Saraf as a focal point. Second, read your selection. Third, enter into a dialogue as a member of a dyad or small group. The following five steps and subtopics will guide you through the process.

Step One: Awareness

Collaborators become aware that gender equity is clearly a moral issue in either of these narratives. Explain the violations of human rights in these narratives. Are there moral opportunities that call for involvement by Christians?

1. Identify gender equity issues in the narrative.
2. Identify components of the gender equity issues.
3. Seek relevance of the whole and parts (i.e., to culture, society, religion).
4. Seek implications to persons and their cultures (e.g., applications to time, place, resources).

Step Two: Metalog and Metacognition

This is a quiet period where collaborators reflect on the content of the narrative (metalog). In addition, group members reflect on their thinking process (metacognition).

1. Be aware that internal thought discourse is ongoing.
2. Reflect on *how* one is thinking.
3. Reflect on the "ethno-cultural" lens through which one is thinking.

Step Three: Inquiry

Share the questions that pertain to the group process, your thought processes, and those issues raised in the narrative. In what ways is the need for gender equity being framed?

1. Hold in check critical judgment when asking or listening to different types of comments and questions.
2. Use culturally appropriate nonverbal and language patterns when generating and asking questions.
3. Plan follow-up questions for clarification purposes if thought helpful.
4. Use a culturally appropriate interview format when interacting with colleagues.

Step Four: Reflection on and Extraction of Transcendent Values or Wisdom Principles

Transcendent values are those principles that extend beyond person, place, time, or situation.

1. Listen and reflect with deliberation.
2. Explore thought processes.
3. Identify central concepts or wisdom principles.
4. Compare similar perspectives.
5. Contrast differences in perspectives.
6. Extract transcendent values or wisdom principles that apply to gender equity.

Step Five: Advocacy Presentation

Present verbal or graphic reports relating to the findings of the preceding five-step critical reasoning process.

1. Share how your position addresses the gender equity issues.
2. Communicate clearly your position or positions.
3. Request feedback as to how your position or positions are understood.

4. Share the transcendent values or wisdom principles relating to gender equity and propose how these might be applied in other settings.
5. Give reasoned support for future advocacy opportunities.

Advocacy: Concluding Thoughts

Advocacy requires us to be sensitive to the heritage and cultural transmission in which feminists live. In nations that do not separate matters of religion and state, there may be few safety nets to protect feminists. For example, during summer school, I and three other women formed a study group to clarify the abstract principles of advanced statistics. Malika's cultural roots were in Iran, Egypt was the home to Sanna, and the remaining two of us held United States passports. Our cultural roots were different. Jamika was an African American woman, and I had been born in India to parents of Pentecostal missionaries. As we bonded, I was urging my Middle East sisters to import creativity and critical thinking into their homeland's educational system. In a voice heavy with emotion and tears welling up in her beautiful dark eyes, Malika responded, "Would you have me sacrifice my son?"

SUMMARY AND CONCLUSIONS

Social justice for the emancipation of women in religious, political, and socioeconomic venues requires Christians to show advocacy in leadership when addressing moral injustices. Although the Bible has been interpreted to support gender inequality, readers can find evidence that God does not discriminate between women and men.

When violations of gender equity occur, Christians have a moral responsibility to work towards a fair and just resolution. One approach is participating in mediated learning dialogues. Compacts for equality provide another progressive approach. These endeavors assist in understanding that moral issues have multiple dimensions, and through reasoned interactions we can progress toward a more equitable and socially just society.

If you choose to join this campaign for gender equality, expect stalwart opposition from the patriarchal gatekeepers who protect thousands of years of opposition. Their misconduct clothed in self-righteousness supposedly bestowed by Creator God will attempt to thwart those working for social justice.

Western, secular societies have passed laws and instituted policies to protect gender equality, but under the protection of religious freedom, Christian groups continue to maintain beliefs and practices indicating that women are intellectually and morally lesser creations. This belief is a hoax. Since women have had access to education and advanced opportunities, they have demonstrated habits of the mind and habits of the spirit equal to that of their male counterparts. Certainly it is time that our religious lives become more holistic, inclusive, and dedicated to justice-focused ways.

I close this chapter with a poem, "Listening Here," by Mark Richardson, who was one of my students. He articulates the complexity found in intergenerational continuity and change.

> Listening here, today
> I have been each of you and
> Another and
> My family, also.
> Who am I now, then?
> I am each of you, as your
> Speech creates me.
> I am another, as my
> Hearing destroys me.
> And I am my family, also,
> As I assume the quiet
> Mind of my ancestors.[16]

ADDITIONAL RESOURCES

The following references were not cited in the text but are included for interested readers.

Carter, Jimmy. *A Call to Action. Women, Religion, Violence, and Power.* New York: Simon & Schuster, 2014.

---

16. Richardson, "Listening Here," February 16, 1991.

Feuerstein, Shmuel. *Biblical and Talmudic Antecedents of Mediated Learning Experience Theory*. Jerusalem: International Center for the Enhancement of Learning Potential, 2002.

General Conference of the Methodist Church. *Social Principles of the United Methodist Church 2009–2012*. Washington, DC: United Methodist, 2009.

Gundry, Patricia. *Women Be Free*. Grand Rapids: Zondervan, 1977.

Hunt, Mary E. *New Feminist Christianity. Many Voices, Many Views*. Woodstock, VT: Skylight Paths, 2010.

Jeansonne, Sharon P. *The Women of Genesis: From Sarah to Potiphar's Wife*. Minneapolis: Fortress, 1990.

Kozulin, Alex. *Psychological Tools: A Sociocultural Approach to Education*. Cambridge, MA: Harvard University Press, 1998.

Lindley, Susan Hill. *You Have Stept out of Your Place: A History of Women and Religion in America*. Louisville: Westminster John Knox, 1996.

Mollenkott, Virginia Ramey. *The Divine Feminine: The Biblical Imagery of God as Female*. New York: Crossroad, 1991.

Narayan, Uma. *Dislocating Cultures: Identities, Traditions, and Third World Feminism*. New York: Routledge, 1997.

Talaska, Richard H. *Critical Reasoning in Contemporary Culture*. Albany: State University of New York Press, 1992.

Winter, Miriam Therese. *WomanWord: A Feminist Lectionary and Psalter: Women of the New Testament*. New York: Crossroad, 1990.

REFERENCES

American Association of University Women. "AAUW Issues: Sexual Harassment and Sexual Violence in School." Accessed June 17, 2016. http://www.aauw.org/what-we-do/public-policy/aauw-issues/sexual-harassment-violence-in-school/.

Feuerstein, Reuven, et al., eds. *The Dynamic Assessment of Cognitive Modifiability*. Jerusalem: International Center for the Enhancement of Learning Potential, 2002.

George Washington University. "Sexual Harassment." Accessed June 17, 2016. https://haven.gwu.edu/sexual-harassment.

Miller, Robert J. *The Complete Gospels: Annotated Scholars Version*. Sonoma, CA: Polebridge, 1994.

Swan, Laura. *The Forgotten Desert Mothers*. New York: Paulist, 2001.

Wiseman, Carol. "Lament of the Daughters." In *Encyclopedia of Pentecostal and Charismatic Christianity*, edited by Stanley Burgess, 201. New York: Routledge, 2006.

10

Tensions and Challenges: Christian Morality and Sex Education

April Montoya and Shonna Crawford

"I THINK I'M READY to start having sex with my boyfriend." These were the words that a fifteen-year-old girl so confidently stated as I drove her home after youth group on a Wednesday night. I was completely caught off guard and at a loss for words. My husband and I had been youth pastors for only two short years, and this girl had been a part of our youth group for most of that time. I thought, "Did she really just say that to a pastor's wife?" But all I could manage to say out loud in response was, "Oh really? Why do you think you're ready?" Immediately, I regretted the question, wishing I had instead said something more holy, something that reflected my Christian values. This smart, hard-working young lady answered my question very matter-of-factly by explaining that she and her boyfriend had been dating for almost a year and that they were in love. And then she told me that she wanted to have sex with him so that he would know she loved him, and hopefully not break up with her. While she seemed perfectly happy at the thought of beginning a sexual relationship for this reason, I could not wrap my mind around the fact that this beautiful, intelligent girl sitting beside me could make such a foolish decision. She did not see the heartache that lay before her, or the possibilities of contracting an STI or getting pregnant. She did not see how this decision might change how others view her, how he saw her, or how she perceived herself. She did not know that this one decision, though it seemed logical, had the potential to impact every future romantic relationship. I wondered where we had failed in youth ministry, and why we hadn't talked more about sexuality with our teens. I knew that the high school she attended required sex education in its health classes and utilized an abstinence-based curriculum. But it became very evident during my conversation with her that she had not been provided with the necessary tools to make this decision. Her perception of sexuality appeared to be primarily based upon how popular culture and media displayed sex.

It was after this conversation that I (April) realized teenagers did not view sex or sexuality in the same way that I did when I was a teen. A lot changed since I was growing up, and it was naïve of me to assume that a regular church youth group attendee would understand and follow Christian values regarding sexuality. Because I was raised by parents with strong biblical morals, I had developed an idea that, though they may not always act accordingly, Christians overall understood biblical standards for sex. It was disappointing to realize that this was not the case, and this experience broke through the misperception I had about teens and sex. I could no longer bury my head in the sand and ignore the topic.

THE NEED FOR SEX EDUCATION

Parents, educators, single adults, and adolescents are faced with many moral challenges when thinking about how to approach sexuality. The teen pregnancy rate in the United States has steadily declined since its peak in the 1990s, with teen pregnancy rates decreasing by 51 percent between 1990 and 2013.[1] While this is good news, and the Centers for Disease Control (CDC) believes the decline to be the result of a national push for sex education, the U.S. still holds the highest teen pregnancy rate among most developed countries, including Canada and the United Kingdom.[2] According to a recent study, 65 percent of U.S. high school seniors reported that they had had sexual intercourse, and 34 percent said they were currently sexually active. This study also showed that one-in-six high school students admitted to having sex with four or more partners, and almost 40 percent did not use a condom during their last sexual encounter.[3] Educators, policy makers, and curriculum directors from various states have mandated sex-education curriculum for public school classrooms. In the United States,

1 "Trends in Teen Pregnancy."
2. Ibid.
3. Barr et al., "Improving Sexuality," 397.

twenty-five states require all sex-education programs in public schools to stress abstinence, and twelve states require all sex-education programs to cover abstinence but not necessarily stress abstinence rather than contraception use. Eighteen of those states and Washington, DC, require that sex-education programs include contraception information.[4] We are living in a world where it is unwise and unfeasible for Christian educators and parents to avoid the discussion about sexuality with teens, specifically adolescents in sixth grade and up.

WHAT SHOULD TEENS LEARN FROM SEX EDUCATION?

Although most parents, educators, and others working directly with teens, sixth grade and up, would agree that sex education is beneficial for adolescents, what should be taught is still a controversial topic. Central to this controversy are two opposing views: (1) that sexuality is intended solely for marriage, and (2) that sexuality may be experienced outside a marriage commitment and that this choice is highly individualistic, devoid of influence by God or any other authority. Because Christian morality aligns with God's standards for sexuality, Christians often find themselves purposefully, or unintentionally, opposing those who do not hold a Christian worldview.

In addition to concerns about Christian morality, Christians can also find the selection of sex-education methods challenging. Abstinence-only and information-based methods are the two primary schools of thought regarding sex education.[5] In this chapter we will compare these two methods utilized in U.S. public schools: *Abstinence Only Until Marriage* (AOUM) and *Comprehensive Sexuality Education* (CSE). We will also discuss how Christian morality is an essential component of any sex-education program. Although our focus is on early sex-education programs for adolescents, many components are also important for single adults.

1. Abstinence Only Until Marriage (AOUM)

The AOUM method heavily emphasizes abstinence as the central component of sex education. Sometimes abstinence is simplified, assuming that

---

4. Ibid., 398.
5. Lamb, "Just the Facts?," 443.

TENSIONS AND CHALLENGES: CHRISTIAN MORALITY AND SEX EDUCATION

teaching teens to "just say no" will be sufficient to curb all sexual urges. AOUM methods view sex as a temptation to do wrong: abstinence is right and premarital sex is wrong. CSE methods leave out the element of temptation and instead present sex as morally neutral: neither right nor wrong. The AOUM method argues that providing specific information about sexual activity will only encourage adolescents to engage in sex before marriage, and it aims to educate solely on delaying sexual activity in order to prevent pregnancy and Sexually Transmitted Infections (STIs), Sexually Transmitted Diseases (STDs), and/or Human Immunodeficiency Virus (HIV).[6] The goal of AOUM methods is to prevent adolescents from engaging in sexual activity.

2. Comprehensive Sexuality Education (CSE)

The CSE method, on the other hand, claims that educating about all areas of sexual health, including proper use of birth control, pregnancy termination, and abstinence, is the solution to preventing teens from engaging in what this method refers to as *risky* sexual behavior, including various sex acts without the use of a condom, sexual activity before age eighteen, multiple sex partners, and trading sex for money or drugs. CSE methods leave out the element of temptation and instead present sex as morally neutral, neither right nor wrong. CSE assumes teens will choose to have sex. Expecting them to resist is impractical and archaic. The goal of CSE methods is to provide tools for "safe sex" or "safer sex" and to reduce risky adolescent sexual behavior.[7]

TENSIONS: THE CHRISTIAN AND SEX EDUCATION

Simply by looking at AOUM and CSE methods, we see how easily tensions arise when selecting or teaching a sex-education method. The tensions exist because the major approaches to sex education fail to provide a comprehensive Christian approach to sex education. For example, in selecting one of the major approaches, Christians may select a method that may not be consistent with Christian morality but has shown more positive results

6. Barr et al., "Improving Sexuality," 398.
7. Lamb, "Just the Facts?," 443.

in reducing risky adolescent behavior. An additional source of tension is deciding how to present biblical principles as the foundation for healthy sexual behavior.

Christian parents and educators most often align the AOUM method of sex education with their Christian morals simply because it invites morality to be a part of the discussion of sexuality whereas the CSE method often ignores morality. While both methods contain some effective elements, neither truly takes into account the cultural and spiritual influences that are deeply intertwined with sexuality. Sadly, research does not confirm that either of these methods has completely succeeded in preventing adolescents from engaging in unbiblical sexual behavior. In addition, neither method encourages something we believe is critical—a cultural shift that allows teens to view sexuality from a holistic perspective.

Outcomes of Sex-Education Methods

Through methods such as True Love Waits and other abstinence education initiatives, approximately 2.5 million teens nationwide have made public declarations to remain abstinent until marriage.[8] While research has shown that teens who participated in these methods did delay their first sexual experience, approximately 88 percent of them eventually participated in premarital sex. Research has also shown that AOUM methods have put adolescents at a higher risk for pregnancy and STDs than those who have participated in CSE methods.[9]

CSE methods have shown better results in reducing *risky* adolescent sexual behavior. For example, studies have shown a link between CSE methods and decreased teen pregnancy rates, delayed sexual debut, increased condom use,[10] and decreased number of sexual partners.[11] Comparing effective outcomes of AOUM and CSE methods reveals that CSE methods initially reduce *risky* adolescent sexual behaviors, but these effects begin to disappear within six months to two years after CSE education takes place.[12] One apparent flaw in CSE methods is that they fail to address and change

---

8. King and King, *True Love Project*.
9. Freedman-Doan et al., "Faith-Based Sex," 250.
10. Kendall, *The Sex Education Debates*, 12.
11. Collins et al., *Abstinence Only*, 8.
12. Kendall, *The Sex Education Debates*, 11.

the driving forces behind adolescent sexual behavior, including values, parenting, and popular culture.[13]

Although evidence supports the relative effectiveness of the CSE approach, Christian sex educators and parents need moral principles consistent with biblical guidance about sex and relationships. Methods such as CSE can change in response to cultural values and lifestyles, but adolescents and their parents need approaches founded on durable principles of Christian morality. When parents do not have a foundation supporting their decisions, they may be hindered in their ability to communicate and enforce sexual guidelines with their children.[14]

Social and Cultural Influences

A school classroom is not the only place teens receive messages about sexuality. Sex-education methods are not addressing social and cultural influences adequately. Nancy Kendall states, ". . . We see that CSE and AOUM approaches often result in quite similar consequences despite their hotly contested ideological differences. We see that, as with all arenas of school policy and practices, the messages that students receive about sex and sexuality may not always be those that are expected or desired."[15] Teens receive messages about sexuality every day through TV, music, Facebook, Twitter, Instagram, and other social media sites. The most-watched TV series during the 2013–2014 season was *The Big Bang Theory* with 23.1 million viewers.[16] The show contains numerous sexual references in each episode.[17] Contrary to Christian morality, sexuality is displayed in a casual manner, and sex before marriage is normalized. The show displays one-night stands, casual sex, or sex without any type of commitment, and the idea that masculinity derives from sexual conquest. Characters frequently move from one sex partner to the next, and an overly sexualized lifestyle is normalized. Unbiblical sexual behavior occurs without negative consequences. *The Big Bang Theory* and other programs are teaching teens a form of sexuality that is not founded upon biblical morality. Although their aim is entertainment and not education, teens learn about sexuality.

13. Ibid., 12.
14. Jones and Jones, *How and When*.
15. Kendall, *The Sex Education Debates*, 15.
16. Schneider, "America's Most Watched."
17. Leon, "The Cinderella Scientist," 6.

Until sex educators discover or create an effective, holistic sex-education program, Christians will experience tension. For Christians, a sex-education program must teach values consistent with biblical morality. But Christian morality is not enough because Christian youth need skills to combat the negative cultural and social influences. Effective sex-education programs also require an evaluation component. Ongoing evaluation not only helps educators determine the effectiveness of the program as a whole, but evaluation also allows educators to modify various components of the program.

ESSENTIAL COMPONENTS OF EFFECTIVE SEX EDUCATION

In this section, we identify the components needed for an effective, holistic sex-education program that is both comprehensive in scope and consistent with Christian values. We begin by reaffirming the importance of a biblical basis for sex education. Researchers find many teens agree that morals, values, and/or religious beliefs significantly influence their decisions to engage in or abstain from sex.[18] Although we list Christian morality as a separate component, we integrate this component into each of the others to demonstrate how Christian moral principles explicitly inform effective sex education.[19] In the subsections below, we introduce the essential components of a sex-education program provided in the following list.

Six Essential Components of Effective Sex Education

1. Christian Morality: How Christian values influence and inform the content of sex education.

2. Healthy Relationships: How do respect, trust, boundary-setting, and communication skills promote healthy relationships? What ways can couples experience intimacy apart from sexual activity?

3. Media Literacy: How to filter and interpret media and its messages about sexuality.

---

18. Collins et al., *Abstinence Only*, 9.

19. To read more about a Christian view of sexuality, see the booklet "Theology of Sex" by the National Association of Evangelicals.

4. Abstinence: Why waiting will create the most fulfilling relationship.
5. Risks: What are the risks of STIs, STDs, HIV, and pregnancy?
6. Contraceptives, abortion, and emergency contraceptives (the morning-after pill): What are they, and how do they work? Why do contraceptives fail to protect against hurt, shame, disappointment, tension, or guilt?

Components of Healthy Relationships

Discussion about what constitutes healthy relationships must be the platform upon which Christians approach and teach sex education. This allows both sociocultural and moral aspects of sexuality to be addressed. Given the messages provided by popular culture, Christians cannot assume that teens understand the nature of a healthy relationship. According to *Safe Dates*, an evidence-based teen dating violence prevention curriculum, one in three students between the ages of twelve and eighteen will experience dating violence.[20] To reduce the occurrence of dating violence, including emotional, physical, and sexual abuse, teens must recognize characteristics of healthy relationships such as respect, trust, boundaries, and communication. Sexuality can only be handled appropriately when these characteristics are present. Equipping teens with the tools to develop healthy friendships and dating relationships will produce an environment for making good decisions about sex. According to the World Health Organization, "Sexual health is a state of physical, emotional, mental, and social well-being . . . not merely the absence of disease, dysfunction, or infirmity."[21]

First Corinthians 13:4–7 describes love in a way that is beneficial when developing healthy relationships. It explains that "love is patient, love is kind. It does not envy, it does not boast, it is not proud. It does not dishonor others, it is not self-seeking, it is not easily angered, it keeps no record of wrongs. Love does not delight in evil but rejoices with the truth. It always protects, always trusts, always hopes, always perseveres" (New International Version).

Here are some questions to ask to promote discussion about sexuality within a healthy relationship: What is my motivation for wanting to have sex? Am I manipulating my partner? Have I discussed personal and

---

20. Foshee and Langwick, *Safe Dates*.
21. Higgins et al., "Sexual Satisfaction," 1643–54.

sexual boundaries with my partner? Am I pressuring my partner to engage in sexual activity that he/she is not comfortable with? Is my partner pressuring me?

Media Literacy

The media heavily influence adolescents in their decisions involving sexuality. Teaching media literacy is vital in sex education. According to a recent study, "The SMD (Sexual Media Diet) measure showed a significant association with adolescents' sexual activity and future intentions to be sexually active, with measures of movie and music showing the strongest associations."[22] Christian parents and educators may feel the need to shelter or protect teens from being exposed to sexuality in the media, and although there is some wisdom in keeping teens from viewing sexually explicit content, media can be used as a stimulus to promote discussion and education. Romans 12:2 says, "Do not conform to the pattern of this world, but be transformed by the renewing of your mind. Then you will be able to test and approve what God's will is—his good, pleasing and perfect will" (NIV). Teaching teens to think critically about what commercials, TV shows, movies, music, magazines, and advertisements are communicating about sexuality will help them to separate healthy messages from unhealthy ones. Discussion can be formed around the fact that characters in TV shows and movies are not real, so they do not need to work through the emotional components of sexual activity the same way a real person would. These questions may promote critical thinking about media: What is valued in entertainment/advertisement? Are men and women valued as people or simply sex objects? Why does entertainment/advertisement display sexuality the way it does? Is it simply because sex sells? Do they care about the people who are consuming their products?

Abstinence.

For Christians who believe the Bible is clear that sexual immorality causes harm and destruction, supporting abstinence is easy. In 1 Corinthians 6:16, Paul speaks directly about the bonding or unity that occurs as a result of sex, stating, "the two will become one flesh" (NIV). Remaining abstinent

---

22. Pardun et al., "Linking Exposure," 75–91.

until marriage allows this bonding to occur easily in marriage. The biblical solution to sexual temptation and the harm that accompanies sexual immorality is marriage: "But because of the temptation to sexual immorality, each man should have his own wife and each woman her own husband."[23] However, abstinence and early marriage are often unpopular decisions among adolescents. Christians must present biblical standards about sexuality along with tools to navigate the messages of a sexualized culture, remembering that "just say no" is not sufficient in abstinence education. In 1 Corinthians 6:12, Paul says, "'I have the right to do anything,' you say—but not everything is beneficial" (NIV). Teens have the choice, whether parents and teachers like it or not, to participate in sexual activity. Teens need to know that while this is ultimately their choice, being sexually active before marriage is not inviting God's best for their lives.

The CDC affirms that the safest practice of sexuality is in a long-term, mutually monogamous relationship.[24] Marriage is the long-term, mutually monogamous relationship that God provides. The bonding that takes place in marriage is what allows sexuality to be the most fulfilling, where trust develops over time, and a lifetime commitment provides security. Instead of approaching abstinence from a negative perspective, reinforcing the "no, no, no" mentality, teens can be taught that abstinence is a positive decision, and that marriage provides the best, most fulfilling, and safest sexual experiences.

The following questions may invite exploration of the benefits of abstinence: What are my personal life goals, and will having sex get me closer to accomplishing those goals? What do I want my future marriage relationship to be like? Will being sexually active now help or harm my future marriage? Will I regret waiting to have sex until marriage?

STIs/STDs/HIV/Pregnancy

According to CDC data from 2013, 67 percent of reported chlamydia infections and 56 percent of reported gonorrhea infections occurred among fifteen- to twenty-four-year-olds.[25] While Christians may be hoping to avoid this possibly embarrassing and graphic topic, teens must understand the reality and risk of contracting STIs, STDs, and HIV and becoming pregnant

---

23. 1 Cor 7:2 (NIV).
24. Centers for Disease Control and Prevention, "Mutual Monogamy."
25. Ibid., "Reported STDs," 1–3.

when engaging in premarital sexual behavior. Information should be provided about the different types of infections and diseases, the symptoms (or lack of symptoms), the temporary and permanent effects, and treatments available for each. In the same report, the CDC also stated that "both young men and young women are heavily affected by STDs — but young women face the most serious long-term health consequences. It is estimated that undiagnosed STDs cause 24,000 women to become infertile each year."[26] So, while these elements need to be discussed as prevention, they are also essential for helping those who have already engaged in *risky* sexual behavior, who may need information and community resources.

The following questions may challenge teens and single adults to consider the harm associated with premarital sex: How would contracting an STI, STD, or HIV change my life and my future relationships? How would getting pregnant change my life and my future relationships?

Contraceptives

As stated previously, neglecting to include information about contraceptives and abortion in sex education has been linked to increased rates of births to teenage mothers. Most Christian traditions view abortion as its own moral issue (distinct from the moral issues regarding premarital sex), and the Catholic tradition views contraception as an independent moral issue. Unfortunately, even with a strong Christian moral foundation, many will not remain abstinent until marriage. While Christians do not want to condone or give permission for teens to engage in premarital sex, information about contraceptives is important. Singles and married couples need to know about the types of contraceptives, how they work, and their effectiveness. Contraceptives are not 100 percent effective in preventing pregnancy, and depending on the type of sexual activity, contraceptives are not 100 percent effective in preventing the transmission of STIs, STDs, and HIV. More importantly, contraceptives do not protect against the regret, hurt, or shame that often accompany premarital sex. The Department of Family and Consumer Sciences at Southwest Texas State University conducted a study of college students and found that guilt was the number one reason why young women did not physically enjoy their first time having sex.[27]

---

26. Ibid., "Reported STDs," 2.
27. Higgins et al., "Sexual Satisfaction," 1643–54.

Sex education should also include information about abortion: what it is, how many weeks into a pregnancy an abortion can legally be performed (this varies by state), the medical complications and risks, the community resources that are available as alternatives to abortion, and the moral concerns.[28] Information should also be provided about emergency contraceptives, more commonly known as the "morning-after pill." Both of these contraceptive methods can have lasting emotional effects, and both have significant moral implications given the belief that life begins at conception, a position held by many Christians. God knows people while they are still in the womb and has designed their existence from the moment of conception.[29] When Christians approach contraceptives and abortion from the perspective described in this section, teens can gain valuable information for a future marriage relationship and understand the importance of waiting to engage in sexual activity.

The following questions will encourage consideration of the pros and cons of contraceptives: What do contraceptives *not* protect against? Will I experience emotional, social, and/or spiritual harm if I engage in sexual activity? Would I ever want to be put in a situation where I have to make a decision about abortion? Within a marriage relationship, are all contraceptive methods acceptable, or do some end the development of a person's life?

WHAT/HOW TO ADDRESS ISSUES FROM A BIBLICAL PERSPECTIVE

It is no secret that a percentage of teens in Christian churches are sexually active. According to *Relevant Magazine*, 80 percent of evangelical Christians admit to having premarital sex. The article also states that, according to a Gallup poll, 76 percent of evangelical Christians believe that premarital sex is "morally wrong."[30] There appears to be a significant gap between Christian moral teaching and what Christians actually do. Although many teens believe they should abstain from sex, many do not achieve this goal. Some believe the Christian church as a whole has not handled sexuality discussions in a healthy way and that the main message being communicated to teens is "just say no." Learning ways to say "no" to sexual activity is important, but for many it is not a sufficient control strategy to overcome sexual desire,

28. For a lengthy discussion of abortion issues, see chapter 7.
29. Ps 139:13, 15; Ps 22:10–11; Gal 1:15.
30. Charles, "(Almost) Everyone's Doing It."

the "just say yes" messages from the surrounding culture, and other sources of social influence. "Just say no" messages identify sex as a forbidden fruit, often creating an even greater appeal and excitement for teens.

Another problem with the "just say no" approach is the implied message that sex and sexuality are negative, which can make it difficult to think positively about sexuality after marriage. "No, no, no" messages link shame and guilt to sex, which is not always easily removed after the wedding when the message instantly turns into "yes, yes, yes."

In addition to making the decision to remain abstinent until marriage, singles may consider what types of sexual activity, if any, are appropriate until marriage. Is holding hands ok? What about kissing or making out? The following questions may serve as a guide for determining personal boundaries: Would I do this in front of my parents? Would I be comfortable talking to my parents about this? Do I need to hide this from others? Am I having any doubts that this is right? Would I be offended or hurt if my future spouse did this with someone else?

Because it is natural and God-designed for people to desire intimacy, singles need to know that choosing abstinence will create loneliness at times. They need reminders that no person or relationship can fulfill their needs for intimacy like a connection with God. In 1 Corinthians 7, the Apostle Paul writes that he wishes all people could remain single/abstinent as he was. He explains that those who choose to be in an intimate relationship will experience hardship and pain because the needs and desires of their spouse will be a priority. He suggests that those who can should remain single, saying that those who do can fully devote themselves to a relationship with Christ. Abstinence among singles is not popular, but if they can experience and understand the fulfillment that comes from intimacy with Christ, it can provide a strong foundation on which to stand for abstinence until marriage.

It is important to remember that even for those who chose to participate in sexual activity before marriage, abstinence and biblical sexuality can still be experienced. Despite engaging in unbiblical sexual behavior, all have the ability to start over, decide to remain abstinent until marriage, and re-establish sexual boundaries. Most importantly, singles should know that there is grace and forgiveness for their mistakes. In 2 Corinthians 5:17, Paul explains the grace that is received when a person seeks forgiveness: "Therefore, if anyone is in Christ, he is a new creation. The old has passed away; behold, the new has come" (ESV, English Standard Version). While singles who have previously engaged in unbiblical sexual activity may find it more difficult to refrain, it is not impossible. In 1 Corinthians 10:13, Paul explains that God provides sufficient grace: "No temptation has overtaken you that is not common to man. God is faithful, and he will not let you be tempted beyond your ability, but with the temptation he will also provide the way of escape, that you may be able to endure it" (ESV).

ADDITIONAL RESOURCES

1. Spoken word about sexuality from a Christian perspective: https://www.youtube.com/watch?v=peea_WkumfQ.
2. Magazine article on sexuality from a Christian perspective: http://www.relevantmagazine.com/life/relationships/almost-everyones-doing-it.
3. A sex-education program that helps students understand sexuality based upon biblical principles: http://www.elifenetwork.com/education-for-a-lifetime/.
4. The "Theology of Sex" booklet is available from the National Association of Evangelicals at http://nae.net/theology-of-sex/.

DISCUSSION QUESTIONS

1. How does a Christian student, parent, or educator evaluate and select sex education when it does not match—or, worse yet, conflicts with—their personal morality?
2. Should a student participate in a sex-education program even if the curriculum goes against biblical teaching? Should parents allow their child to participate in such a program?
3. Should a Christian educator teach a required curriculum that contradicts biblical morality?

REFERENCES

Barr, Elissa M., et al., "Improving Sexuality Education: The Development of Teacher-Preparation Standards." *Journal of School Health* 84 (2014) 396–415.
Charles, Tyler. "(Almost) Everyone's Doing It." *Relevant* 53 (2011). Accessed June 17, 2016. http://www.relevantmagazine.com/life/relationships/almost-everyones-doing-it.

Centers for Disease Control and Prevention. "Mutual Monogamy." http://www.cdc.gov/std/prevention/.

———. "Reported STDs in the United States: 2013 National Data for Chlamydia, Gonorrhea, and Syphilis." December 2014. Accessed June 17, 2016. http://www.cdc.gov/std/stats13/std-trends-508.pdf.

Collins, Chris, et al. *Abstinence Only vs. Comprehensive Sex Education: What Are the Arguments? What Is the Evidence?* San Francisco: AIDS Research Institute, 2002.

Fohee, Vangie, and Stacey Langwick. *Safe Dates: An Adolescent Dating Abuse Prevention Curriculum.* 2nd ed. Center City, MN: Hazelden Information & Educational Services, 2010.

Freedman-Doan, Carol R., et al. "Faith-Based Sex Education Programs: What They Look Like and Who Uses Them." *Journal of Religion and Health* 52 (2013) 247.

Higgins, Jenny A., et al. "Sexual Satisfaction and Sexual Health among University Students in the United States." *American Journal of Public Health* 101, no. 9 (2011) 1643–54.

Jones, Stan, and Brenna Jones. *How and When to Tell Your Kids about Sex: A Lifelong Approach to Shaping Your Child's Sexual Character (God's Design for Sex).* Carol Stream, IL: Nav, 2007.

Kendall, Nancy. *The Sex Education Debates.* Chicago: University of Chicago Press, 2013.

King, Clayton, and Sharie King. *True Love Project: How the Gospel Defines Your Purity.* Nashville: B&H Kids, 2014.

Lamb, Sharon. "Just the Facts? The Separation of Sex Education from Moral Education." *Educational Theory* 63 (2013) 443–60.

Leon, Alexis. "The Cinderella Scientist: A Critical Reading of the CBS Series, 'The Big Bang Theory.'" *Media Report to Women* (2014) 6.

Pardun, Carol J., et al. "Linking Exposure to Outcomes: Early Adolescents' Consumption of Sexual Content in Six Media." *Mass Communication & Society* 8, no. 2 (2009) 75–91.

Schneider, Michael. "America's Most Watched: The Top 50 Shows of the 2013–2014 TV Season." *TV Guide*, June 6, 2014. Accessed June 17, 2016. http://www.tvguide.com/news/most-watched-shows-2013-2014-1082628/.

"Trends in Teen Pregnancy and Childbearing." U.S. Department of Health and Human Services, June 2, 2016. Accessed June 17, 2016. http://www.hhs.gov/ash/oah/adolescent-health-topics/reproductive-health/teen-pregnancy/trends.html.

11

Morality in Local and Global Perspectives

PAUL W. LEWIS

"WHERE DID MY BRUSH go?" "It is over here," was the reply. "What is it doing over there?" "I used it this morning," was the second person's response. The first voice demanded, "Why did you steal my brush? I thought that you were a Christian." This was met with stunned shock. Although somewhat truncated, this kind of conversation inevitably occurred at least once a trimester at Asia Pacific Theological Seminary in Baguio, Philippines, where at any time there were about twenty or more nationalities represented among the student body. As the Academic Dean (from 2006 to 2012), I encountered even more serious concerns. Typically, the first speaker was from one of the Western countries and had a heightened view of personal ownership. Such a person would not have had a problem with the brush being used if first asked. Their dorm mates in this scenario were from Asia or the Pacific Islands. As such, they would assume, since they are roommates, "what is yours is mine" and vice versa.

Over the last two decades, especially while we lived in Asia, we have continuously asked questions like these: What is the relationship between ethics and culture? Are there universals and moral absolutes, as some Christian ethical theorists espouse, or is there a cultural or moral relativism as many contemporary anthropologists and humanists endorse? Or is there a mediating path, allowing both universals and cultural-relative aspects while affirming elements of both? In this chapter, I will endeavor to chart out a mediating path of conduct between cultural-moral relativism and universal moral absolutism when looking at intercultural ethics.

While I think it is possible to argue universal and local elements of ethics in general,[1] I will presuppose a Christian perspective, and therefore I will include theological considerations about universal and local ethics.

CULTURE AND ETHICS

By *culture* I mean "the web of significance human beings weave in order to create meaning."[2] Culture includes a complex conglomerate of customs, knowledge, beliefs (philosophical, religious, and other), worldviews, habits, conduct and rituals, which have a form of internal coherence, and assumed acceptance. Culture is not only a sum of these elements collectively; it also includes the rationality of how things make sense within the culture.[3] Further, culture is paradigmatic in the sense that all information is filtered and put together a certain way through the lens of a presupposed paradigm.[4] Culture is a dynamic enterprise where, in one sense, humans are formed by the culture, and they are a part of (especially if born and raised in) that culture. Yet the capacity of people to reach beyond themselves also means that people play a role in shaping their own culture.[5] In recent years, growing globalization and urbanization have demonstrated more clearly the dynamic element of culture as cultures interact, change, adopt, adapt, and/or re-entrench in our contemporary world.[6]

---

1. For example, Cacciatore, "Intercultural Ethics."

2. Deifelt, "Intercultural Ethics," 112. Deifelt is interacting with Geertz, "Thick Description," 5.

3. Rationality is about how the thought process operates or flows within cultural-linguistic groups; Augsburger, *Conflict Mediation*, 28–35. See also Nisbett, *The Geography of Thought*; and, as a foil, see Ong, *Orality and Literacy*.

4. I will follow Kuhn's concept of paradigm, which originates in *The Structure of Scientific Revolutions* (1962), yet, due to criticisms of the vacillating definition of *paradigm* (e.g., Masterman, "The Nature," 61–66), his revised edition (1970) and later work (*The Essential Tension*, 292–319; *The Road Since Structure*, 13–32) greatly refine this term, and others use *paradigm* and note the epistemological filter component (e.g., Barbour, *Myths, Models, and Paradigms*, 95–98; Masterman, "The Nature," 76–79; Ratzsch, *Philosophy of Science*, 45–56). I have discussed Kuhn's use of *paradigm* elsewhere in more detail: Lewis, "The Baptism," 302–3.

5. Some would call it to "transcend themselves"; Deifelt, "Intercultural Ethics," 112.

6. Ibid., 112–19.

Ethics is interested in what is good or right. In particular, ethics focuses on what people *ought* to do rather than just what they do. In the field of ethics, there are three prominent ethical or moral systems: teleological, deontological, and virtue or character ethics.[7] Teleological ethics focuses on the goal, or *telos*, so attaining the desired result is considered what is right or good. Deontological ethics determines rightness based on duties, and rules, so obeying the rules, respecting a person's rights, or following one's obligations is what is good or right. Virtue or character ethics is more focused on moral agents themselves (i.e., "being precedes doing"), so good character is the primary focus, and conduct derives from that. In terms of a cross-cultural ethics, Bernard Adeney argues that, of these three systems, character ethics best allows for cultural distinctions with the acceptance of universal elements.[8] Embedded in any of the ethical systems is the engagement of moral dilemmas, the process of making moral judgments (i.e., moral decision-making), the determination and application of moral conduct, and the manner of the formation of morality within a person or group.

In the first two sections of this chapter, I will argue for the truth of both universal elements and cultural (and personal) differences. The third section will emphasize certain theological considerations for an intercultural ethics, and the final section will delineate certain facets of an intercultural ethics that includes both global and local engagements in making moral decisions.

GLOBAL/UNIVERSAL CONSIDERATIONS

In the West, a form of universal ethics was common in the medieval period through the theological suppositions of universality of creation, God, and sin. However, with the rise of the Enlightenment, rationalism highlighted a different kind of universalism. For instance, Immanuel Kant proposed the Categorical Imperative, which was an innate moral foundation found in every human. Notably, in the last half of the twentieth century there has

---

7. Adeney, *Strange Virtues*, and Tyra, *Pursuing Moral Faithfulness*, divide the ethical systems the same way while other ethicists divide the systems differently (e.g., Hudson, *Modern Moral Philosophy*), but all cover the same basic areas. In chapter 2, Brandon Schmidly makes the same distinction, using the term *consequentialist* instead of *teleological*.

8. Adeney, *Strange Virtues*, 26–27.

been a strong rejection of universal ethics linked to the role of the colonial powers. In the colonial period, it was assumed that the colonial culture (whether European, U.S., or Japanese) was the "right culture." Therefore, its rules were to be followed. The "rightness" (whether cultural, religious, or ethical) of the colonial culture was linked to its power. Thus, ethical determinations did not consider local cultural sensitivities. Rather, the colonial power's rule, desire, and power informed the local cultures and ethical practices.[9] The cultural imperialism that accompanied the colonial emissaries (e.g., missionaries, medical personnel, Foreign Service workers), while mostly unintentional, perpetuated a presupposed "superior" cultural self-identity (e.g., to dress up in coat and tie for formal occasions even in tropical countries). In the post-colonial perspective, it is common to reject the "cultural imperialism" and, by association, any affirmation of universal values in favor of endorsing equal and independent cultural identities.

In international business and management, the discussion about universal concerns runs headlong into the concern for diversity of management needed in cross-cultural contexts. Geert Hofstede and his colleagues observe that there may be value continuums common to all cultures, but diversity and differences between cultures is paramount.[10] Likewise, in the social science literature, some researchers highlight universal concerns, needs, and capacities found in all of humanity, but equally note personal and cultural differences.[11]

Directly tied to the post-colonial rejection of universality noted above is the standard position in contemporary postmodern thought that there are no absolutes. The quest for certainty is dead. Instead of absolutes and certainty, there is a variety of legitimate positions or "truths." Pluralism or relativism is foundational to postmodernity. Statements like, "Jesus Christ

---

9. One example was the British power to enforce the opium trade in China even while Chinese leadership opposed this. I understand that this was a complex economic and political issue, but for a fine work sorting through this with an emphasis on the missionary opposition to the opium trade, see Lodwick, *Crusaders against Opium*.

10. Hofstede, *Culture's Consequences*; and Hofstede, Hofstede, and Minkov, *Cultures and Organizations*; those that follow: House et al., *Culture, Leadership, and Organizations*; and Lewis, *When Cultures Collide*.

11. On social-science literature, e.g. Kluckhohn, "Universal Categories of Culture," and Malinowski, *A Scientific Theory of Culture, and Other Essays*, 91–119; On universal, cultural, and personal elements, see Augsburger, *Pastoral Counseling Across Cultures*, 48–78; and *Conflict Mediation across Cultures*, 11–41; and Kluckhohn, Murray, and Schneider, *Personality in Nature*.

is Lord of All" are rejected.[12] In short, in the postmodern mindset, the possibilities of any universal truth or metaphysical statement are rejected.

Paradoxically, some common universals are promoted in contemporary societies (e.g., human rights, democracy, and market economy).[13] The recognition of cultural diversity and differences, does not preclude consideration of that which is common and universal.[14]

LOCAL/CULTURAL CONSIDERATIONS

Culture is the filter through which meaning flows to a person.[15] Certain aspects of culture are embedded and embodied. Embedded aspects of culture include such presupposed elements as language, worldview, collective beliefs, and other modes of communication (e.g., nonverbal). Embodied aspects of culture are those that are lived out in life—physically, emotionally, mentally, and socially in a shared rationality. Some universal aspects of culture reflect biological and psychological commonalities (e.g., need for food and shelter, need for esteem).[16] Other commonalities can be placed on continuums: power distance, uncertainty avoidance, individualism, masculinity versus femininity, long-term orientation, and indulgence versus restraint.[17] Life is always seen through the lens of culture, and even universals are historically situated for the observer.[18] For instance, reading this chapter requires a knowledge of English and a certain level of education. These are all culturally defined and historically situated.

When looking at cultures, we must use caution when comparing "universals" of culture because there is a tendency to equate phenomenological similarity with sameness. Clifford Geertz calls these "fake universals" since concepts such as religion or marriage appear the same but function very

---

12. There are many works on this topic, but I will highlight my summary of postmodernity; Lewis, "Postmodernity and Pentecostalism," 38–43.

13. These three are from Immanuel Wallerstein's work, *European Universalism*, noted in Cacciatore, "Intercultural Ethics," 26; Benhabib, *The Claims of Culture*, 24–48.

14. Cacciatore, "Intercultural Ethics," 34.

15. There are many good works on cultural anthropology; I have interacted with Grunlan and Mayers, Cultural Anthropology; and Hiebert, *Cultural Anthropology*; and works by Lingenfelter (e.g., *Transforming Culture*) and Kraft (e.g., *Christianity in Culture*) among others.

16. Augsburger, *Pastoral Counseling*, 50–58.

17. This is the core of Hofstede's work.

18. Cacciatore, "Intercultural Ethics," 30.

differently in one culture compared to another.[19] Differences can be further refined based on variations due to familial, subcultural, and personal influences.[20] In other words, while there are universals common to being human (most notably based on biological and psychological foundations),[21] and cultural elements do provide meaning, humans can also transcend their cultural upbringing to act counter-culturally.[22] Understanding the complexity of a culture can be difficult in a cross-cultural situation, especially when a missionary or foreign worker interacts primarily with one local person to obtain insight into cultural behavior, habits, rationality, or any other aspect of culture. In any culture, a particular person may actually reflect only their personal views or those of their family rather than adequately or accurately representing the variations in the entire culture.

Cultural differences are often viewed from the perspective of cultural relativism. According to strong relativism, all cultures have equal value, and ethical principles are equally valid; however, not all social scientists agree with strong relativism, which is critical of basing any ethical decisions on an absolute.[23]

A final issue is the problem of commensurability most evident in concerns about effective communication. If cultures are independent of one another (i.e., incommensurable), then how can people from different cultures communicate? If they can communicate at least at a minimal level, how effective is that communication? And can they communicate on matters of ethics? A strict incommensurability between cultures is clearly false.[24] In reality, when communication occurs, there is "a moral danger in insisting too glibly and rapidly upon total commensurability."[25]

---

19. Geertz, "The Impact," 49, brought to my attention by Augsburger, *Pastoral Counseling*, 67–68.

20. Interestingly, J. R. R. Tolkien notes this distinction in his narratival description of hobbits; see Lewis, "Tolkien as Ethnographer." This also highlights a danger found in many biblical cultural books based on biblical stories. One reference from a narrative should not be evidence for a cultural norm. It may be a personal decision or a familial habit without necessarily being a cultural norm.

21. E.g., Augsburger, *Pastoral Counseling*, 50–58; Malinowski, *A Scientific Theory of Culture*, 91–119; note also Maslow's hierarchy of needs is based on this concept.

22. Augsburger, *Pastoral Counseling*, 63–65; and Goff, "Cross-Cultural Ethics," 58–59.

23. Cacciatore, "Intercultural Ethics," 27–28.

24. Benhabib, *The Claims of Culture*, 29–33; and Duty, "Doing Christian Ethics," 49–50.

25. Ibid., 31.

An awareness of commensurability with an acceptance of some loss of understanding in cross-cultural communication or "weak relativism" should be acknowledged.[26] Furthermore, a common response in international business is that while it is certainly true that there is great diversity among cultures, awareness of the potential to cross these differences is assumed.[27] Further, interreligious and intercultural dialogues, as well as the whole missions enterprise is based on the premise that there is some degree of commensurability between cultures.

THEOLOGICAL CONSIDERATIONS

In Christian theology, one core belief is that God is the creator. This implies a universal order and an intelligent design. In addition, humanity was intentionally created by God in the image of God.[28] Christian theologians have understood this special creation in a variety of ways. And they ask whether sin has tainted, totally distorted, or minimally impacted, if at all, the *imago dei*. However, regardless of different perspectives, the consensus view is that every human reflects the image of God.[29] As such, there are universal facets embedded in all of humanity.

Although theologians endorse universal aspects of creation in general as well as universal aspects of being created in the image of God, they acknowledge problems accessing these universals for two reasons. First, humans, unlike God, have limited knowledge relevant to understanding facts pertinent to identifying a universal.

Sin is the second reason for the difficulty in recognizing universal aspects of creation. Since the Protestant Reformation, theologians have emphasized that sin is so pervasive that humanity is totally depraved. Thus, people cannot see or comprehend the universal truths represented in God's creation.

Some argue that culture is a result of sin;[30] I will argue that culture is part of being human. Cultures have good, bad, and neutral elements.

---

26. Ibid., 33–42; and Cacciatore, "Intercultural Ethics," 27–28.
27. E.g., Harris and Moran, *Managing Cultural Differences*.
28. Theologians often use the term *imago dei* to mean "created in the image of God."
29. Harris and Moran, *Managing Cultural Differences*, 469–74, 494–509.
30. While Kraft (*Christianity in Culture*) assumes the possibility of having forms in cultures that are neutral, Lingenfelter (*Transforming Culture*) propounds that, since humanity is steeped in sin, all cultures exude that sinfulness and thus there are no "neutral"

Humans make decisions, and while persons are informed by their culture, they are also influencers of their culture and can even operate outside their cultural norms at a familial or personal level.[31] Biblically, it can be seen that while some cultures certainly can become more sinful than others (e.g., Sodom and cities that did not receive the disciples of Jesus), in general, cultures are treated ambiguously.[32]

While affirming universal aspects of creation, there should also be an affirmation of the diversity in creation. Sex differences (male and female) are affirmed as good and only good together (man/male was not good alone).[33] Diversity (in creation) is good. In fact, in Revelation 7:9–10, John notes that there will be people from every language and every tribe singing praises to God. The differences are affirmed biblically within the context of following God.[34] Yet this diversity of peoples, languages, and cultures in the framework of worshiping God is seen as the eschatological certainty and desired end.

The Tower of Babel story highlights cultural-linguistic separation (from other cultures) due to sin.[35] Theologically, the corporate sin of hubris was the cause of the cultural-linguistic division, which led to differences in moral values. Cultural or moral relativism is based on the Tower of Babel divisions. The Acts 2 (Day of Pentecost) and Acts 10 ("Gentile Pentecost") events demonstrated a reversal of the cultural-linguistic separation.[36] This latter point is important in that there is a clear affirmation of the overcoming of the cultural-linguistic divisions endemic since the Tower of Babel. This reversal of the separation also has moral ramifications. Since Acts 2, God's Spirit has provided a way to overcome the separation linked to the sin reflected in the Tower of Babel story.

---

elements in a culture. So while I am summarizing my position, I am fully cognizant of the Kraft-Lingenfelter-Hiebert interactions/debates on this topic.

31. Augsburger, *Pastoral Counseling*, 48–78.

32. Sherlock, *The Doctrine of Humanity*, 129–33.

33. Gen 2:18.

34. See for example, Ruth (the Moabite) and Rahab (the Canaanite) who were both ancestors of Jesus and clearly noted in Matthew's genealogy of Jesus in Matt 1. It could be argued that the Revelation passage is due to redemption and thus not necessarily creation. For the purposes of this essay, I will assume that diversity is promoted through creation and redemptively assured eschatologically.

35. Gen 11.

36. Lim, "Acts 10"; Dulles, *Catholicity*, 173; Sherlock, *The Doctrine of Humanity*, 144; Volf, *Exclusion and Embrace*, 226–31; Wenk, *Community-Forming Power*, 256.

Other passages from Acts 2, 6, and 10 demonstrate the inclusion of historically different cultures (e.g., Hebraic Jews versus Hellenistic Jews; Jews versus Romans/Gentiles), Also, in Acts 15, the council of Jerusalem decided that Gentiles do not have to become Jews in order to be followers of Jesus. So, biblically, diversity and cultural differences are affirmed, but for Christians, the incommensurability between cultures is ultimately denied (at least through the Spirit).

To summarize the theological considerations, diversity is a natural part of the created order, but there are also differences due to sin. It is important not to equate personality, familial customs, or cultural differences as necessarily sinful. However, sin can lead to the strengthening of intercultural divisions, strife, and disputes. All humanity—every culture—can be influenced and divided by sin. However, each can be guided to the redemptive reality in Jesus Christ, which can overcome sin and cultural distance. Each culture has insights and perspectives that the others do not have. Culturally, it means that a multilateral (not just bilateral) approach is needed to ethically engage the globalized world. In 1 Corinthians 12, Paul argues that there are many members in one body. In the West, we have typically argued that this is about individuals within a church; I would also suggest that the verse can apply to cultures and nations. To paraphrase, the Jews cannot say to the Greeks, I have no need of you, or the Romans to the Africans, I have no need of you.

INTERCULTURAL ETHICS

A Christian intercultural ethics starts with the premise that there are universals and absolutes that can be affirmed (e.g., the primacy of Christ for salvation in Philippians 2:5–11) while allowing for cultural (as well as familial and personal) differences. There are three ways a universal principle is accepted while allowing for diversity. First, Christian ethics focuses on the centrality of God and Jesus Christ. "Every culture and person must change in light of a new perspective—Jesus Christ, crucified, risen, and exalted."[37] Or, as L. Gregory Jones notes about the Trinitarian aspect of ethics, "On

---

37. Lingenfelter, *Transforming Culture*, 18. It is hard to read Bonhoeffer's *Cost of Discipleship* without being completely challenged by his commitment to Christ and following him, as Bonhoeffer states, "When Christ calls a man, he bids him come and die," 99. You can see this primacy of Christ in many of his other works as well (e.g., *Ethics*; *Christology*) as the heuristic key for ethics and all of life.

this Christian account what is important is not only formation but *transformation in moral judgment*" (author's emphasis).[38] Second, differences and diversity, which can be part of the created order, do not necessarily equate with sin. And third, the universal message of the Bible is to everyone both individually and corporately.

For individual Christians, God communicates ethics in three ways: through the Bible, through the community, and by direct communication.[39] The impact of the Bible is through hermeneutically sound methods, attitudes, and perspectives, which are informed by the communal influence of traditional understanding. The community informs an individual's ethics through dialogue. The individual identity or self is formed and transformed, both within a point in time and over time (i.e., progressively).[40] Second, in theological ethics, a robust theological method includes the guidance of the Holy Spirit in the formation of the Bible within the parameters of consensus throughout church history.[41] This historical process involves the universal church, which includes influences that vary in terms of different cultures throughout the world as well as variations in time. Ultimately, these broad influences occur in connection with local churches. Third, in addition to individuals acting as moral agents (i.e., making moral judgments and practicing moral conduct), the community of faith (the church) also functions as a moral agent. It is impossible to isolate the personal from the church community.[42] Fourth, ethics is formed from the past through tradition moving narratively as an unfolding story into the future being pulled by vision while coherently situated in embodied practices. All four aspects of formation (tradition, vision, narrative, practices) are necessary for holistic ethical development.[43] Fifth, and related to community, is the importance of friends and friendships to forming one's ethics.[44] The close-

38. Jones, *Transformed Judgment*, 75.

39. Lewis, "A Pneumatological Approach."

40. Such as through God speaking to us directly or through decisions; such as through discipleship or personal development (i.e., moral developmental psychology).

41. For a consensual approach to Christian theology, see Oden, *After Modernity... What?*, 160–63; and Oden, *Word of Life*, ix–xxi. This is spelled out in more detail in Lewis, "A Pneumatological Approach."

42. Deifelt, "Intercultural Ethics," 112–19.

43. There is a vast amount of material on this; I recommend that you look at the ethical writings of Craig Dykstra, Stanley Hauerwas, L. Gregory Jones, Alisdair MacIntyre, and Gilbert Meilander among many others.

44. Clearly seen in Aristotle's *Nicomachean Ethics*; and more recently in Jones,

ness of friendship informs and stretches the individual toward greater or worse moral actions.

When exegeting the Bible, analyzing the historical perspectives, and engaging cross-culturally, there needs to be an attitude of humility, peacemaking, and openness.[45] This process requires times for reflection both theological and relational, individual and communal, within a culture and across cultures. Biblical, theological, personal, and social analyses are needed for continued growth. Further, for the intercultural Christian and any missionary, the attitudes and practices should exude service. Reflection guides and helps the person evaluate himself or herself accordingly.

The interculturally aware Christian lives cross-culturally, transculturally, and counter-culturally.[46] Cross-cultural communication can take place at four levels of moral discourse: at the mores level (basic customs), at the moral level (deeper questions), at the reflective underpinnings level (basis of moral decisions), and at the metaphysical and epistemological foundations level.[47] Only with the right attitude and a full depth of discourse can intercultural ethics develop. Christians engage transculturally when they connect in those areas that are universal (thus, the importance of social concern which connects at the common human level). All Christians are also to be counter-cultural. Allegiance to the Kingdom of God requires all Christians to be critics of their own culture. Likewise, cross-cultural workers (outsiders) who cannot fully understand the culture like an insider can provide insight into an insider's "blind spots." Thus, there will always be a need for missionaries in any culture.[48]

One of the basic components of an intercultural ethics is the idea that principles transfer but practices do not. If a practice happens to transfer, it may have more to do with an accident of history or globalized (or even colonial) forces, or it may not be genuine sameness. Further, there are times that a practice may transfer but the understanding of the practice may differ. Thus, for many in a pluralist or interreligious view of global ethics, the

---

Transformed Judgment; and Wadell, *Friendship*.

45. Humility is noted by Deifelt, "Intercultural Ethics," 118; peacemaking by Goff, "Cross-Cultural Ethics," 64; and openness as "stepping outside ourselves . . . imaginatively" to cross social boundaries, taking "the other into our own world," and repeating the process by Duty, "Doing Christian Ethics," 50–51, taken from Volf, *Exclusion and Embrace*, 250–53.

46. On all three, see Goff, "Cross-Cultural Ethics," 56–59.

47. Kelly, "Cross-Cultural," 314–15.

48. Ibid., 312–13.

focus is not on the moral principles but on the common practices or issues (e.g., human trafficking).[49] This highlights the need for discernment to identify universals and apparent common practices as well as how to engage people having common goals despite different moral presuppositions.

Ethical development takes place when people are close, engage in dialogue, and become mirrors to one another. This process allows people to see themselves as others do and to see their own potential.[50] As Christians, this closeness also reflects Christ-in-us, which has clear ethical dynamics. Dialogue in a cross-cultural setting includes the heart-to-heart engagement beyond a mere surface conversation in order to overcome vast cultural differences. As such, the relationship between the persons must be close enough to discuss concrete issues and to hear what the other really thinks, not just what one may believe the other desires to hear. The dialoguers should also have cultural awareness and sensitivity, cross-cultural communication skill, and an open mindset. In many parts of the world, when the relationships are at the surface level, responses to inquiries are frequently based on "saving face" or not causing shame. It takes both cultural-linguistic acumen and closeness to connect at a deeper level and learn what another really thinks. Implied in this is the cross-cultural openness and understanding to have genuine friendship "with symmetrical participation."[51] The goal is not imposing sameness, which can be imposed internally or externally. A goal of genuine openness to the other is foundational to dialogue, intercultural ethics, and following Christ as one embracing the other.[52]

From the above discussion, it is possible to endorse universal moral affirmations (e.g., God is good) without being a moral absolutist. Likewise, one can endorse cultural differences and diversity without subscribing to a moral relativism. A biblically based, Spirit-led engagement with intercultural ethics allows for a diversity of persons within and between various cultures to interact with authentic dialogue polycentrically (many members within a culture, and across many cultures).

---

49. Three works in this desire for global ethics, but from different methodologies and slightly differing perspectives on the universal while looking at common ground, are Crawford, *World Religions*; Küng, *Global Responsibility*; and Wolfe and Gudorf, *Ethics & World Religions*. Note that Küng's project elicited a great deal of reactions in journal responses and interactions.

50. Niebuhr, *The Responsible Self*, 69–89. The Bible likewise can function as a mirror reflecting the person as they are / can be and God (with both holiness and grace).

51. Deifelt, "Intercultural Ethics," 112.

52. Ibid., 112–19; and Volf, *Exclusion and Embrace*.

CONCLUDING REMARKS

I started this essay with a personal story and will end with the same. Over the years in Asia, I developed many wonderful friendships. Once, in Asia, I was in a meeting with several members of various cultures. An ethical issue came up for discussion. An American said, "We will do this because this is what the locals do." The response of the two who were from there was, "That is what non-Christians do; we as the national church do not do that." Later, my wife and I visited with both individually (with their respective spouses), I could sense the anger toward the original statement, the hurt, and the disbelief regarding the original comment. As we talked, I found different perspectives and rationalities for the ethical issue involved, but as I opened up to listen to their understanding of the Scripture, church history (including local), and ethical understanding, I found myself appreciating their approach in general, and especially the local context/situation. I found myself reevaluating my own perspective and ethics. In this case and at other times, my perspective and resulting moral decision-making and judgments changed. At other times we did not ultimately agree, but I could see their point, and we could continue to work together with respect and understanding. However, just as often, they told me their perspective or moral judgment changed from our time together. The polycentric engagement happened at times when we had an intercultural dialogue with representatives of other cultures in our community, Western and Asian. Frequently, we arrived at a consensus. But at other times we agreed on an ethical principle, but a local expression was needed in terms of acceptable conduct. A functional and flourishing intercultural ethics is possible, but it must be intentional, and at times we must have a high tolerance for ambiguity.

ADDITIONAL RESOURCES

1. You can learn more about Hofstedt's approach to understanding culture at this website: http://geert-hofstede.com/.
2. A helpful summary of *Culture and Cognitive Science* can be found in the *Stanford Encyclopedia of Philosophy*. http://plato.stanford.edu/entries/culture-cogsci/.
3. Christians are concerned about human trafficking. It is a moral problem that cuts across several cultures. Several articles can be found

at Christianity Today. http://www.christianitytoday.com/ct/topics/h/human-trafficking/.

DISCUSSION QUESTIONS

1. Based on the information in this chapter and considering the additional resources, write and discuss a definition of *culture*.
2. What is the relationship between ethics and culture?
3. Discuss the problem of applying universal moral principles to similar problems in different cultures. You can read more about moral relativism in *Stanford Encyclopedia of Philosophy* at this web address: http://plato.stanford.edu/entries/moral-relativism/.

REFERENCES

Adeney, Bernard T. *Strange Virtues: Ethics in a Multicultural World*. Downers Grove, IL: InterVarsity, 1995.
Alston, William. *Perceiving God*. Ithaca, NY: Cornell University Press, 1991.
Augsburger, David W. *Conflict Mediation across Cultures: Pathways and Patterns*. Louisville: Westminster John Knox, 1992.
———. *Pastoral Counseling across Cultures*. Louisville: Westminster John Knox, 1986.
Barbour, Ian. *Myths, Models, and Paradigms*. San Francisco: HarperCollins, 1974.
Benhabib, Seyla. *The Claims of Culture: Equality and Diversity in the Global Era*. Princeton: Princeton University Press, 2002.
Bonhoeffer, Dietrich. *Christology*. Translated by John Bowden. London: Harper & Row, 1966.
———. *The Cost of Discipleship*. Translated by R. H. Fuller. Rev. ed. New York: Macmillan, 1963.
———. *Ethics*. Edited by Eberhard Bethge. New York: Macmillan, 1965.
Brainard, F. Samuel. "Defining 'Mystical Experience.'" *Journal of the American Academy of Religion* 64 (1996) 359–93.
Cacciatore, Giuseppe. "Intercultural Ethics and 'Critical' Universalism." *Cultura: International Journal of Philosophy of Culture and Axiology* 8, no. 2 (2011) 23–38.
Carson, D. A. *Christ and Culture Revisited*. Grand Rapids: Eerdmans, 2008.
Crawford, S. Cromwell, ed. *World Religions and Global Ethics*. New York: Paragon House, 1989.
Danto, Arthur. "Ethical Theory and Mystical Experience: A Response to Professors Proudfoot and Wainwright." *Journal of Religious Ethics* 4 (1976) 37–46.
———. *Mysticism and Morality*. New York: Basic, 1972.
Deifelt, Wanda. "Intercultural Ethics: Sameness and Otherness Revisited." *Dialog: A Journal of Theology* 46, no. 2 (2007) 112–19.
Dulles, Avery. *The Catholicity of the Church*. Oxford: Oxford University Press, 1987.

Duty, Ronald W. "Doing Christian Ethics on the Ground Polycentrically: Cross-Cultural Moral Deliberation on Ethical and Social Issues." *Journal of the Society of Christian Ethics* 34, no. 1 (2013) 41–63.
Erickson, Millard J. *Christian Theology*. 3rd ed. Grand Rapids: Baker Academic, 2013.
Ferraro, Gary. *Cultural Anthropology: An Applied Perspective*. 6th ed. Belmont, CA: Wadsworth, 2006.
Forman, Robert K. *Mysticism, Mind, Consciousness*. Albany: SUNY, 1999.
Forman, Robert K., ed. *The Problem of Pure Consciousness*. New York: Oxford University Press, 1990.
Geertz, Clifford. "The Impact of the Concept of Culture on the Concept of Man." In *The Interpretation of Cultures: Selected Essays by Clifford Geertz*, 33–54. New York: Basic, 1973.
———. "Thick Description: Toward an Interpretative Theory of Culture." In *The Interpretation of Cultures: Selected Essays by Clifford Geertz*, 3–30. New York: Basic, 1973.
Gill, Jerry. "Wittgenstein and Religious Language." *Theology Today* 21 (1964) 59–72.
Goff, Bill. "Cross-Cultural Ethics for World-Class Christians." *Southwestern Journal of Theology* 42, no. 2 (2000) 45–64.
Grunlan, Stephen A., and Marvin K. Mayers. *Cultural Anthropology: A Christian Perspective*. Grand Rapids: Zondervan Academie, 1979.
Hardy, Douglas. "Implicit Theologies in Psychologies: Claiming Experience as an Authoritative Source for Theologizing." *Crosscurrents* 53 (2003) 368–76.
Harris, Philip R., and Robert T. Moran. *Managing Cultural Differences*. 3rd ed. Houston: Gulf, 1991.
Hauerwas, Stanley. *A Community of Character*. Notre Dame: University of Notre Dame Press, 1981.
———. *The Peaceable Kingdom*. Notre Dame: University of Notre Dame Press, 1983.
Hay, David. "Religious Experience amongst a Group of Post-Graduate Students: A Qualitative Study." *Journal for the Scientific Study of Religion* 18 (1979) 164–82.
Hay, David, and Ann Morisy. "Reports of Ecstatic, Paranormal, or Religious Experience in Great Britain and the United States: A Comparison of Trends." *Journal for the Scientific Study of Religion* 17 (1978) 255–68.
Hiebert, Paul. *Cultural Anthropology*. Grand Rapids: Baker, 1983.
Hofstede, Geert. *Culture's Consequences: Comparing Values, Behaviors, Institutions, and Organizations across Nations*. London: Sage, 2000.
Hofstede, Geert, Gert Jan Hofstede, and Michael Minkov. *Cultures and Organizations: Software of the Mind*. 3rd ed. New York: McGraw-Hill, 2010.
Holmes, Arthur F. *Ethics: Approaching Moral Decisions*. Downers Grove, IL: InterVarsity, 1984.
House, Robert J., et al., eds. *Culture, Leadership, and Organizations: The GLOBE Study in 62 Societies*. Thousand Oaks, CA: Sage, 2004.
Hudson, W. D. *Modern Moral Philosophy*. Garden City, NY: Anchor, 1970.
Jenson, Matt. *The Gravity of Sin: Augustine, Luther and Barth on homo incurvatus in se*. London: T. & T. Clark, 2006.
Jones, L. Gregory. *Transformed Judgement: Toward a Trinitarian Account of the Moral Life*. Notre Dame: University of Notre Dame Press, 1990.
Katz, Steven. "Language, Epistemology, and Mysticism." In *Mysticism and Philosophical Analysis*, edited by Steven Katz, 22–74. New York: Oxford University Press, 1978.

———. "Responses and Rejoinders: On Mysticism." *Journal of the American Academy of Religion* 61 (1993) 751–57.
Katz, Steven, ed. *Mysticism and Philosophical Analysis*. New York: Oxford University Press, 1978.
———. *Mysticism and Religious Traditions*. Oxford: Oxford University Press, 1983.
Kelly, David C. "Cross-Cultural Communication and Ethics." *Missiology: An International Review* 6, no. 3 (1978) 311–22.
Kluckhohn, Clyde. "Universal Categories of Culture." In *Anthropology Today: Selections*, edited by Sol Tax, 304–20. Chicago: University of Chicago Press, 1962.
Kluckhohn, Clyde, Henry A. Murray, and David M. Schneider. *Personality in Nature, Society, and Culture*. Rev. ed. New York: Knopf, 1956.
Kraft, Charles. *Christianity in Culture*. Maryknoll, NY: Orbis, 1981.
Kuhn, Thomas. *The Essential Tension*. Chicago: University of Chicago Press, 1977.
———. *The Road since Structure*. Chicago: University of Chicago Press, 2000.
———. *The Structure of Scientific Revolutions*. Rev. ed. Chicago: University of Chicago Press, 1970.
Küng, Hans. *Global Responsibility: In Search of a New World Ethic*. New York: Crossroad, 1991.
Küster, Volker. "Intercultural Theology Is a Must." *International Bulletin of Missionary Research* 38, no. 4 (2014) 171–76.
Lindbeck, George. *The Nature of Doctrine*. Philadelphia: Westminster, 1984.
Lingenfelter, Sherwood. *Transforming Culture: A Challenge for Christian Mission*. 2nd ed. Grand Rapids: Baker Academic, 1998.
Lewis, Paul W. "The Baptism in the Holy Spirit as Paradigm Shift." *Asian Journal of Pentecostal Studies* 13, no. 2 (2010) 301–44.
———. "A Pneumatological Approach to Virtue Ethics." *Asian Journal of Pentecostal Studies* 1, no. 1 (1998) 42–61.
———. "Postmodernity and Pentecostalism: A Survey." *African Journal of Pentecostal Theology* 1 (2003) 34–66.
———. "Tolkien as Ethnographer: The Role of Culture in J. R. R. Tolkien's *The Lord of the Rings*." In *What's So Liberal about the Liberal Arts?*, edited by Paul W. Lewis and Martin Mittelstadt. Eugene, OR: Pickwick, forthcoming.
———. "Toward a Pentecostal Epistemology: The Role of Experience in Pentecostal Hermeneutics." *The Spirit & Church* 2, no. 1 (2000) 95–125.
Lewis, Richard D. *When Cultures Collide*. London: Brealey, 1999.
Lim, Yue Chuen, "Acts 10: A Gentile Model for Pentecostal Experience." *Asian Journal of Pentecostal Studies* 1, no. 1 (1998) 42–61.
Lodwick, Kathleen L. *Crusaders against Opium: Protestant Missionaries in China, 1874–1917*. Lexington: University Press of Kentucky, 1996.
Malinowski, Bronislaw. *A Scientific Theory of Culture and Other Essays*. Chapel Hill: University of North Carolina Press, 1944.
Margolis, Robert, and Kirk Elifson. "A Typology of Religious Experience." *Journal for the Scientific Study of Religion* 18 (1979) 61–67.
Masterman, Margaret. "The Nature of a Paradigm." In *Criticism and the Growth of Knowledge*, edited by Imre Lakatos and Alan Musgrave, 59–89. Cambridge: Cambridge University Press, 1970.

Nicholson, Michael. "Abusing Wittgenstein: The Misuse of the Concept of Language Games in Contemporary Theology." *Journal of the Evangelical Theological Society* 39 (1996) 617–29.

Niebuhr, H. Richard. *The Responsible Self: An Essay in Christian Moral Philosophy.* New York: Harper & Row, 1963.

Nisbett, Richard E. *The Geography of Thought: How Asians and Westerners Think Differently . . . and Why.* New York: Free, 2003.

Oden, Thomas C. *After Modernity . . . What?: Agenda for Theology.* Grand Rapids: Zondervan, 1990.

———. *The Word of Life.* Vol. 2 of *Systematic Theology.* San Francisco: Harper & Row, 1990.

Ong, Walter. *Orality & Literacy: The Technologizing of the Word.* London: Routledge, 1982.

Osborne, Grant R. *The Hermeneutical Spiral: A Comprehensive Introduction to Biblical Interpretation.* Rev. ed. Downers Grove, IL: InterVarsity Academic, 2007.

Proudfoot, Wayne. "Mysticism, the Numinous, and the Moral." *Journal of Religious Ethics* 4 (1976) 3–28.

———. *Religious Experience.* Berkeley: University of California Press, 1985.

Ratzsch, Del. *Philosophy of Science: The Natural Sciences in Christian Perspective.* Downers Grove, IL: InterVarsity, 1986.

Runyon, Theodore. "A New Look at Experience." *Drew Gateway* 57, no. 3 (1987) 44–55.

———. "The Importance of Experience in Faith." In *Aldersgate Reconsidered,* edited by Randy Maddox, 93–107. Nashville: Kingwood, 1990.

Sherlock, Charles. *The Doctrine of Humanity.* Downers Grove, IL: InterVarsity, 1996.

Shuman, Joel. "Toward a Cultural-Linguistic Account of the Pentecostal Doctrine of the Baptism of the Holy Spirit." *Pneuma* 19 (1997) 207–23.

Taves, Ann. *Fits, Trances, and Visions: Experiencing Religion and Explaining Experience from Wesley to James.* Princeton: Princeton University Press, 1999.

Tyra, Gary. *Pursuing Moral Faithfulness.* Downers Grove, IL: IVP Academic, 2015.

Volf, Miroslav. *Exclusion & Embrace: A Theological Exploration of Identity, Otherness, and Reconciliation.* Nashville: Abingdon, 1996.

Wadell, Paul J. *Friendship and the Moral Life.* Notre Dame: University of Notre Dame Press, 1990.

Wainwright, William. "Morality and Mysticism." *Journal of Religious Ethics* 4 (1976) 29–36.

Wenk, Matthias. *Community-Forming Power: The Socio-Ethical Role of the Spirit in Luke-Acts.* New York: Sheffield Academic, 2000.

Wolfe, Regina Wentzel, and Christine E. Gudorf, eds. *Ethics & World Religions: Cross-Cultural Case Studies.* Maryknoll, NY: Orbis, 2009.

12

Reflections on Christian Morality

GEOFFREY W. SUTTON

AND

BRANDON SCHMIDLY

As we conclude this introductory text on Christian morality, we wanted to provide you with more than a summary by offering some thoughts on how this diverse collection of essays may be used as a guide to making Christian moral judgments. To that end, we begin our reflection with a look at Jesus' familiar summary of God's commandments,[1] which was referenced by several authors. In the first statement, Christians are to completely love God. Thus, any understanding of Christian morality begins with a special relationship—one that is fully committed and grounded in love. The Christian message is, of course, that God loves all people and desires to forgive all for their sins. In short, all have failed to live up to God's view of righteousness or morality. All have lost their relationship with God. We are familiar with the gospel message, but here we emphasize the moral dimension—Jesus offers a path to restored relationship in which sins are forgiven and people are reconnected with God. Morality is a relational concept. Christian morality begins with a right relationship with God.

Jesus' second commandment directs us to love others as we love ourselves. Like the first commandment, this call to love our neighbors is about a relationship. Christians live morally when they remain in a loving

---

1. Mark 12:30–31.

relationship with God and respond to others with love. We recognize, of course, that these general principles still require Christians to thoughtfully discuss the problems of life to ensure they act morally. However, we hope that reminding ourselves of Jesus' commandments helps us focus on a primary purpose of moral conduct, to enhance rather than disrupt relationships with others.

We further observe, contrary to the teaching of some, there is no third commandment to love oneself. There are indeed many lessons about right living that apply to us as individuals, yet any code of ethics focuses on how we ought to conduct ourselves in relationship with others. Maintaining a right relationship with God and others entails certain actions on our part.

PRINCIPLES AND EXCEPTIONS

In Luke 13:10–17, Jesus heals a woman on the Sabbath. From the perspective of the Pharisees, Jesus violated God's commandment not to work on the Sabbath. In response, Jesus cited exceptions to Sabbath work that the Pharisees made—they untied and watered their animals on the Sabbath. He then compared his act of freeing the woman from her bondage to the way the Pharisees treated their animals. For the most part, we are able to live our lives according to familiar rules of right conduct. The biblical commandments prohibiting murder and adultery make sense. Christians and non-Christians accept these moral principles. But from time to time, new problems arise that are not specifically covered in the Bible. For example, Jesus declared divorce to be sin but granted an exception for adultery. The Bible does not include an exception for spouse abuse, but most Christians consider abuse to be another acceptable moral reason for divorce. Both adultery and abuse destroy marriage relationships.

Consistent with our authors, we encourage readers to discover and live by principles consistent with the teachings of Scripture. When it is not clear how to derive a principle from the Bible or how to apply a biblical principle in a given situation, we suggest beginning the process of forming a Christian moral judgment by seeking God's guidance in prayer followed by reading relevant scriptural texts in more than one translation. Then we recommend weighing the evidence offered by those leaders who have examined ways to apply principles to the situation of concern.

In this book you have several essays by Christian authors on contemporary moral issues. Clearly, people can interpret the Bible in different ways, and they can disagree on the importance of select pieces of evidence. As editors, we found that we did not always agree with all of the points made by our authors. As we read their essays, we offered comments and asked questions, which we hoped they would use to improve their essays. Yet even when we disagreed, we did so in a way to find a better answer. You do not have the same opportunity to interact with our authors as we did; however, we encourage you to think critically about their essays. If you have a limited understanding in a particular area, you may feel unable to construct a moral argument that explains why you think differently than did one of our authors. We would like you to know that this difficulty is common. That is, many people may not agree with the moral views of another Christian but feel inadequate to give a detailed explanation supporting the disagreement. Instead of either accepting or dismissing the position of one of our authors or another Christian leader, we encourage you to seek a better answer. In doing so, you may find that you agree with some points but not others.

WEIGHING EVIDENCE

In part one, our authors drew upon their disciplines to illustrate how additional information can help us think about a moral dilemma. In Brandon Schmidly's philosophy chapter, we learned the importance of thinking clearly about moral arguments when attempting to form a moral judgment. He further illustrated how careful reasoning may be applied to thinking clearly about the morality of abortion. In Geoffrey Sutton's psychology chapter, we also learned that many are unaware of the extent to which they rely on feelings and habitual ways of acting rather than careful thinking in response to a moral dilemma. Clear thinking is vital to forming a moral judgment. Although we do not need to ignore those feelings that lead to moral outrage, a Christian moral response requires a consideration of principles and the effects on others when acting on those principles. The facts concerning the disproportionate mass incarceration of African Americans presented by Peter Althouse can evoke moral outrage and motivate Christians to act. Careful thinking is needed to revise laws, policies, procedures, and change underlying attitudes.

Several authors referred to scientific evidence when discussing a moral course of action. We acknowledge that weighing scientific evidence can be difficult when experts disagree either about the quality of the evidence or how to interpret the evidence. The best that most of us can do is something akin to what happens in court. We consider the credentials of expert witnesses, and we assess the quality of their arguments. This process is not easy. Some experts lie, and most of us can be deceived. Nevertheless, we may certainly pray for wisdom and attempt to seek knowledge from experts who have publicly presented relevant facts and cogent arguments. Persuasive talks and discussions have their place, but careful study is easier when we can read and reread moral guidance.

Another difficulty for people not familiar with a scientific approach to knowledge is recognizing that scientific findings are revised when new information becomes available. When scientific evidence suggests a high probability that a particular medication is harmful, it is easy to see that it would be immoral to give that medication to anyone. Similarly, when psychologists or sociologists discover the negative impact of a law or way of living, a moral argument can be made for change. Although the Bible does not explicitly state that women should be treated the same way as men are, the negative impact of discrimination on women is abundantly clear. The evidence of discrimination policies reveals centuries of ill treatment affecting women's general health, economic status, safety, and many other aspects of well-being.

Part 2 of this book is our approach to helping you think about various moral issues by including examples of how scholars integrate Scripture with the weighing of evidence and opinions. These methods are not foolproof, but when we begin our quest with God, we can have confidence that he will guide us into truth.

FACTORS INFLUENCING MORAL JUDGMENT

Several authors provide examples of factors that influence moral judgment. As mentioned previously, in the psychology chapter we learned that our thinking can be influenced by our feelings, habitual ways of behaving, and our physiological state (e.g., sexual attraction, general health). It is hard to think clearly about any matter when we are tired, irritable, or angry. We have a natural tendency to behave as we always have—changing bad habits is not easy. And when we are ill or in pain, it is a struggle to focus our attention on resolving a moral dilemma. When faced with a particularly troubling decision, we can ask ourselves if our thinking is distorted by any of these and other personal factors.

Several authors illustrated how social factors impact our view of morality. This is most obvious in Joel Theissen's sociology chapter. But, as already noted, Peter Althouse also showed how cultural factors are relevant to the high rate of imprisonment of African Americans. In addition, April Montoya and Shonna Crawford identified social factors relevant to sex education. And Ruth Burgess illustrated the problems women face in striving against sociocultural barriers to equality. Finally, Paul Lewis illustrated the importance of considering how diverse cultural values might influence the way we decide how some things are right and others wrong. We hope that an awareness of social factors will help all of us seek to live a moral life that is more consistent with universal Christian principles than the principles of a particular culture or subculture.

OTHER TOPICS

If you look at the chapters in other books on Christian ethics or morality, you will see some familiar topics. Most books include chapters dealing with marriage, sexuality, and divorce. Capital punishment and euthanasia are also frequently appearing topics. Books also reflect the era in which they were written. When people began to care about minorities, editors included chapters on women's rights and race-based discrimination. More recent books include chapters on LGBT issues and climate change. Our view is that any book will be incomplete, so the best approach is to learn how to think Christianly and critically about a few topics and apply that method of integrating Scripture, evidence, and reason to forming moral judgments about additional issues. To help you explore additional topics, we included introductory paragraphs with information on additional resources in the Appendix.

REDEMPTION AND THE MORAL LIFE

Although you are undoubtedly aware of God's love and forgiveness, our experience indicates that many can feel weighed down by feelings of guilt and distress over sin. Some of us may just feel bad that we did not realize until later how the things we have or have not done may have hurt others. Perhaps some of us have had an experience that changed our beliefs about what is right and wrong. Like Paul, we likely wonder why we do not always do the right thing.[2] Thus, we hope readers will find it helpful to recall that God recognizes our imperfections—including our imperfect ability to think clearly—and offers us forgiveness and an opportunity to refocus our efforts to live the moral life.

---

2. Rom 7:15–20.

APPENDIX

Other Morality Topics

GEOFFREY W. SUTTON

AND

BRANDON SCHMIDLY

As NOTED IN OUR chapter on reflections, we have included introductory paragraphs on additional topics you may wish to research in more depth. We will add links to additional resources following each section.

ENDING LIVES

A great deal has been written about euthanasia, capital punishment, and going to war—all acts that result in the ending of a human life. There are several issues for Christians to consider, and we suspect you are aware that Christians disagree on the right course of action.

Euthanasia

Euthanasia is sometimes called "mercy killing" and advocates talk about death with dignity. The situations vary. In some cases, a person appears to be unconscious with their life supported only by medical technology. A family member and medical personnel may discuss when to discontinue the support system. In other cases, a person is fully alert but suffering chronic pain and desires assistance to end his or her life in a painless manner. Some countries or jurisdictions (e.g., a state) have laws allowing people to perform or permit actions that will result in death without being liable for murder. Christians have argued at length about euthanasia.

The Bible does not provide specific guidance in dealing with decisions to end human life. A Christian perspective requires an understanding of biblically supported principles and an understanding of what constitutes life. The general consensus is that God is the author of life and all people are created in the image of God. Essentially, this view entails that decisions about death are off limits for humans whether one is speaking about abortion—the death of an unborn child—or the death of someone after birth. In short, life and death are in God's hands.[1]

Some make moral distinctions based on perceived differences between who takes an active role resulting in death. Some see a moral difference in cases where a person requests assistance to die versus cases where the decision is made by others about an unconscious person. Some also see a difference in the active versus passive nature of the processes resulting in death. For example, is there a moral difference in removing life support and letting a person die versus administering a drug known to cause death? The matter of ending the life of an unconscious person supported by medical equipment is also complicated by matters of personal choice. In cases where a person has declared in advance that they do not wish their lives to be prolonged by artificial means, the person has presumably made a choice. This is contrasted with cases where the wishes of the unconscious person are unknown or where family members are trying to decide what the person would want if she or he could make a decision. If you believe no one has the right to end a life, then questions of choice and ending life support are not relevant.

Christians who support euthanasia argue based on an ethic of love and mercy. They see Jesus acting in ways to relieve suffering. In this view, Christians may act to minimize or end lives marked by pain and suffering. A passive approach grants the dying person's wishes to refuse interventions that prolong life. An active approach includes any act by someone other than the dying person to end life in accordance with the dying person's wishes. An intermediate approach provides the dying person with the means to end his or her own life. Christians supporting euthanasia are aware of the potential for abuse and murder and therefore support laws

---

1. In the past, some Christians thought the sixth commandment (Exod 20:13) prohibiting killing applied to the problem of euthanasia, but most think that text applies to murder.

and policies that include checks and balances to ensure a dying person is treated with respect.

Additional Resources on Euthanasia

1. Catholic teaching: http://www.usccb.org/issues-and-action/human-life-and-dignity/end-of-life/euthanasia/.
2. National Association of Evangelicals: http://www.euthanasia.com/evangel.html.
3. Research from Pew Forum: http://www.pewforum.org/2013/11/21/religious-groups-views-on-end-of-life-issues/.
4. James Rachels on killing and letting die: http://jamesrachels.org/killing.pdf.

Capital Punishment

Christians have argued at length about the morality of capital punishment, a punishment normally reserved for committing murder. A Christian's view on the sanctity of human life is one primary issue to consider. Obviously, if all human life is sacred, and if God is solely responsible for creating and ending life, then Christians cannot support any human act that ends a life, including capital punishment. Those supporting capital punishment have often pointed to the Old Testament laws that include the death penalty, and biblical principles such as "eye for an eye." Many will also appeal to the government's responsibility to bring about justice and note that, in some cases, the only just response is the death penalty.

Those Christians opposing capital punishment emphasize that Christians are not bound by Old Testament laws. Instead, they point to the teachings of Jesus focused on love and mercy, and they note the possibility that all people deserve the opportunity to repent. Christians often add additional arguments based on research. Some arguments focus on a supposed deterrence effect. It is difficult to establish a deterrent effect given the large numbers of people who do not commit murder. Some opposed to capital punishment point to the evidence showing many innocent people have been wrongly executed due to discrimination and human error. At this point, there is reasonable evidence supporting discrimination and error. Many of the people exonerated have been African Americans. Some consider capital punishment to be cruel and unusual punishment. As you might suspect, the concepts of *cruel* and *unusual* are open to debate. Some point to the economic costs of capital punishment. In the United States, the appeals process is lengthy and very expensive; thus, life imprisonment is a better economic alternative. Not only do prisoners live, but tax payers do not have their economic burdens increased.

Additional Resources on Capital Punishment

1. Catholic position: http://www.usccb.org/issues-and-action/human-life-and-dignity/death-penalty-capital-punishment/catholic-campaign-to-end-the-use-of-the-death-penalty.cfm.
2. National Association of Evangelicals: http://nae.net/capital-punishment-2/.
3. Research from PewForum: (Search for the Pewforum website for updates) http://www.pewforum.org/2009/11/04/religious-groups-official-positions-on-capital-punishment/.

Going to War

Christians have participated in religious and secular wars for centuries. Though most would argue that Christians ought to be peacemakers and slow to engage in combat, it appears that only a minority believe it is morally wrong to go to war in all cases. As with other cases of ending life, Christians must decide what it means for human life to be sacred. Some Christians believe they can serve in the armed forces if they are not in combat positions. Of course, by virtue of being in a branch of the armed forces, they still support the overall efforts of their peers engaged in killing. Others feel the need to opt out of military service altogether and, where permitted, choose to serve society in some form of public service. Any resident of a nation is, however, linked to the support of that nation, which has led some Christians to emigrate to other nations where practices regarding war are more closely aligned with their moral values.

Christians supporting military service point to the examples of God's leadership of the Israelite wars in the Old Testament. And they point to Jesus' treatment of a Roman soldier and lack of condemnation for soldiers.[2] Those opposed to military service, especially combat roles, emphasize

2. See Matt 8:5–13; Luke 7:1–10.

God's overall role in life and death decisions as well as Jesus' teachings focused on peace, love, and mercy, noting that Jesus is about restoring life and health—not destroying lives.

Christians and non-Christians have argued about the notion of a *just war*, which implies that some wars may be morally justified and others not. In this debate, you can expect some Christians to cite the opinions of St. Augustine and St. Thomas Aquinas. Over the centuries, those supporting Christians going to war have focused on guidelines essentially limiting killing and destruction to that which is necessary to re-establish peace. Most support the notion that just wars should focus on stopping enemy combatants and destroying resources linked to conducting war. Killing civilians and destroying such facilities as schools and hospitals is not acceptable. In current unconventional warfare, it is not always easy to determine who is and who is not an enemy combatant, and enemy soldiers sometimes use schools and medical facilities as a cover for war-making activities.

Additional Resources on Just War

1. BBC Ethics Resource on Just War Theory: http://www.bbc.co.uk/ethics/war/just/introduction.shtml.
2. Catholic position on Just War: https://www.ewtn.com/expert/answers/just_war.htm.
3. Just War Theory: An introduction in the Stanford Encyclopedia of Philosophy: http://plato.stanford.edu/entries/war/#2.

CARE FOR THE ENVIRONMENT

The issue of the environment is the concern that human activity is changing the environmental conditions so drastically that there will be (and perhaps already are) devastating consequences. Some of the projected consequences include irreversible warming of the planet, rising sea levels that will destroy coastal cities, polluted air and polluted water that will deteriorate human health as well as make irreversible changes in the planet's ecosystem, violent weather, and people's homes becoming uninhabitable resulting in climate change refugees.

When considered as a moral issue, the term *climate change* does not merely refer to a change in the climate. Rather, it is multi-faceted and

APPENDIX—OTHER MORALITY TOPICS

generally implies that the climate is being irreversibly and problematically changed by human activity, and there is something humans can, and should, do about it. There are two unique features of this issue compared to other moral issues. First, climate change is not immediately observable. Matters like war and capital punishment can be observed by everyone, but climate change must be inferred from scientific research. This, by nature of the scientific method, creates opportunity for skepticism about climate change. Those who are skeptical cite evidence that conflicts with climate change theories, accuse researchers of ulterior motives, accuse politicians of advancing climate change as an opportunity to consolidate power, or generally agree with current research but feel the inference of disaster is being hyperbolized.

The second unique feature is that a response to climate change requires collective action rather than individual action or actions by a few. When considering the abortion debate, if one person is convinced to not have an abortion, then there is a real measurable change in the outcomes on the abortion issue (i.e., one less abortion). However, one person deciding to recycle will not make a measurable change in the consequences of climate change. A difference in climate change will require a critical mass of individuals changing their behavior. This may be brought about through public awareness efforts, or perhaps through national and international law.

Christians who advocate for this change may cite biblical passages that reflect God's ownership of the earth. They may also interpret man's dominion over the earth as involving caretaker responsibilities. Even among those who are skeptical about the dangers of climate change, there may be a "better safe than sorry" response to a call for action.

Additional Resources on
Care for the Environment

1. A general resource for Evangelical Christians that includes definitions and links to other resources: http://creationcare.org/.

2. Catholic position on creation care: http://www.usccb.org/beliefs-and-teachings/what-we-believe/catholic-social-teaching/care-for-creation.cfm.

3. Catholic position on climate change: http://www.catholicclimatecovenant.org/.

4. Climate change facts from NASA: http://climate.nasa.gov/evidence/.

5. Information on environmental science including resources: http://www.environmentalscience.org/.

THE NEW RACE RELATIONS

In the 1800s, the world was trading people of other races as they would trade property. Americans who migrated from Europe "owned" people from Africa as slaves. The immorality of this practice eventually brought the United States to war until slavery was abolished. In the 1950s and 1960s, the United States addressed the racist practices of Jim Crow laws. In 2015, several events made it clear that African Americans continue to struggle for recognition and equal rights or protections in the U.S.

The evidence of ongoing struggles comes from several sources. USA Today reported dozens of unarmed African Americans were killed in the past year.[3] Nine people were killed at a Black Church in Charleston, South Carolina.[4] University protests brought issues of race to the international spotlight once again.[5] Although we did not address the specific race issues illustrated in these news stories, you will find an example of moral reasoning about racial issues in Peter Althouse's chapter on theology, where he provides a moral argument for addressing the mass incarceration of African Americans. This type of argument can help you address other issues of racial and ethnic discrimination.

REFERENCES

BBC News. "Protests over Racial Issues Spread to more US Campuses." *BBC News*, November 12, 2015. Accessed June 17, 2016. http://www.bbc.com/news/world-us-canada-34800562.

Horowitz, Jason, Nick Corasaniti, and Ashley Southall. "Nine Killed in Shooting at Black Church in Charleston." *New York Times*, June 17, 2015. Accessed June 17, 2016. http://www.nytimes.com/2015/06/18/us/church-attacked-in-charleston-south-carolina.html?_r=0.

Madhani, Aamer. "Timeline: Dozens of Unarmed African Americans Killed since Ferguson." *USA Today*, August 9, 2015. Accessed June 17, 2016. http://www.usatoday.com/story/news/2015/08/09/timeline-dozens-unarmed-african-americans-killed-since-ferguson/31375795/.

3. Madhani, "Timeline."
4. Horowitz et al., "Nine Killed."
5. BBC News, "Protests over Racial Issues."

RELATED BOOKS BY THE EDITORS

A House Divided
Sexuality, Morality, and Christian Cultures
by Geoffrey W. Sutton
www.wipfandstock.com/a-house-divided-14068.html

Forgiveness, Reconciliation, and Restoration
by Martin W. Mittelstadt & Geoffrey W. Sutton
Available from www.wipfandstock.com

www.ingramcontent.com/pod-product-compliance
Lightning Source LLC
Chambersburg PA
CBHW051741230426
43670CB00012B/2116